KNOW LIGHT NO FEAR

**Understanding Your Faith
and God's Will for Your Life**

Neil ~~~~~~~ n
AND ~~~~~~~

Publishers Since 1798

THOMAS NELSON PUBLISHERS
Nashville • Atlanta • London • Vancouver

Published in Nashville, Tennessee, by Thomas Nelson, Inc., and distributed in Canada by Word Communications, Ltd., Richmond, British Columbia, and in the United Kingdom by Word (UK), Ltd., Milton Keynes, England.

Unless otherwise noted, Scripture quotations are taken from the HOLY BIBLE, NEW INTERNATIONAL VERSION ®. Copyright © 1973, 1978, 1984 by International Bible Society. Used by permission of Zondervan Bible Publishing House. All rights reserved.

The "NIV" and "New International Version" trademarks are registered in the United States Patent and Trademark Office by International Bible Society. Use of either trademark requires the permission of International Bible Society.

Scripture quotations noted NASB are from THE NEW AMERICAN STANDARD BIBLE, Copyright © 1960, 1962, 1963, 1968, 1971, 1972, 1973, 1975, 1977 by The Lockman Foundation and are used by permission.

Scripture quotations noted NKJV are from THE NEW KING JAMES VERSION. Copyright © 1979, 1980, 1982, 1990, 1994, Thomas Nelson, Inc., Publishers.

Scripture quotations noted TLB are from THE LIVING BIBLE (Wheaton, Illinois: Tyndale House Publishers, 1971) and are used by permission.

Library of Congress Cataloging-in-Publication Data

Anderson, Neil T., 1942-
    Know light, no fear / Neil Anderson and Rich Miller.
        p. cm.
    ISBN 0-7825-7663-7 (pbk.)
        1. Spiritual warfare. 2. Fear—Religious aspects—Christianity.
    3. Devil. I. Miller, Rich, 1954- . II. Title.
    BV4509.5.A525 1996
    248.8'3—dc20   95-41524
                                                                    CIP

Printed in the United States of America
1 2 3 4 5 6 7 - 02 01 00 99 98 97 96

To my gentle, caring,
fun-loving wife,
Shirley Grace,
who surely
is a gift of grace
from our Lord Jesus Christ.
Rich Miller

Contents

Part 3: Walking with God

~ Acknowledgments

The adult edition of this book, *Walking in the Light,* was born out of necessity. We had learned how to help people find their freedom in Christ from every conceivable bondage. A core issue in every case was deception. That is why Jesus said, "If you hold to my teaching, you are really my disciples. Then you will know the truth, and the truth will set you free" (John 8:31-32).

The apostle Paul wrote: "The Spirit clearly says that in later times some will abandon the faith and follow deceiving spirits and things taught by demons" (1 Tim. 4:1). That is presently happening all over the world. Many people are in bondage because they are paying attention to deceiving spirits. On the other hand, "those who are led by the Spirit of God are sons of God" (Rom. 8:14). This revised edition of my first book has been written to help younger Christians discern God's guidance in their life and live free in Christ.

I want to thank Rich Miller for all the work he has done to make this revision practical, relevant, and understandable for the younger generation. Rich and his wife, Shirley, are providing tremendous leadership to our college and young adult ministries. I also want to thank Thomas Nelson and their fine editorial staff for seeing the need for such a volume and for the editorial support they have given Rich and me.

All my staff at Freedom in Christ need to be thanked and commended for standing behind us in prayer and for providing all the support services that make a project like this possible. It is a privilege to work with each and every one of you.

It is all these people's prayer and mine that this book will help you live a free and productive life in Christ.

Neil T. Anderson

ᨆᨆᨆ Introduction

s it possible for Christians to be deceived? Absolutely. In our ministry of helping teens and adults find their freedom in Christ, we have often witnessed major deception in the lives of believers. And many of these people are in "full-time" Christian work! "The Spirit clearly says that in later times some will abandon the faith and follow deceiving spirits and things taught by demons" (1 Tim. 4:1).

You've probably witnessed this yourself. How many times have you seen a teenager with a genuine, growing faith in Christ suddenly crash and burn spiritually? Or a faithful youth group attendee suddenly drop out and become apathetic or even negative toward spiritual things? Or a Christian young person make a totally off-the-wall decision that he blames on God?

We must come to grips with the harsh reality that there is a battle going on for our minds and that we can be deceived by the father of lies, Satan (John 8:44). Many times this deception comes through world philosophies such as western rationalism, eastern mysticism, or one of Satan's most current tools, New Age teaching.

New Age teaching and occult religion are as old as the Garden of Eden. What is new is how they're infiltrating every level of society—even the educational system. You may even have had the experience of observing a teacher in your school lead you in relaxation exercises or guided imagery and visualization techniques.

Or you may have been involved in things like "Bloody

Mary," "Ouija," or "Dungeons and Dragons" and thought they were just harmless games—not realizing you may have been opening the door to deceiving spirits.

That's why in part 1 of this book, we'll expose the ways that we can be led astray by counterfeit guidance. We will look at the reasons why our own feelings, intuitions, and thoughts are inadequate guides to discerning the will of God. We'll examine Jesus' warnings about false prophets, false apostles, false teachers, and even false Christs.

We'll talk about how to deal with fear, one of Satan's most effective strategies. We cannot walk by faith while in the grip of fear, so it is essential that we understand the nature of fear and how to overcome it in our lives.

With the rise of Satanism and the increasing influence of New Age beliefs, believers in Christ must become experts in the truth. How else will we be able to recognize the deception of the enemy?

In part 2 of this book we will shift gears and focus on principles for discerning God's will. We will deal with issues like: What is God's will for our lives? How can we know for sure that God is leading us? What does it mean to "walk by faith," and how does the Holy Spirit enable us to tell the difference between the truth and lies?

Part 3 of this book will deal with walking with God. We will see that everything God does in our lives is in the context of His love relationship with us. The key to knowing *God's will* is knowing *God's ways*. And sometimes God's ways are far different from what we would expect.

This is not a book of formulas for mechanically discovering God's will and guidance for your life. It is a book that by God's grace, however, can help you draw near to His presence and follow His leading.

The more you know the truth of God's Word, the better you will be able to walk by faith in Him. The more sensitive you become to the leading of the Holy Spirit, the more accurately you will be able to discern truth from deception.

Unfortunately, we cannot possibly answer every question you have. Some incidents in life are troubling, and we'll simply never know the reasons they occur until we are with Him. We are also deeply aware of the responsibility we bear as authors to not lead anyone astray. So would you read this book prayerfully, looking up the Scriptures we use to see if the things that we write are true?

The Bible is the only infallible source of truth, not Neil Anderson, Rich Miller, or anyone else. We would be arrogant to think otherwise. That's why we have committed ourselves to focusing on God's Word in this book.

If we help keep you from stumbling or wandering off the narrow path of truth in your walk with God, we will be happy. If you are off that path and you come back because of God's truth on these pages, we will be thrilled.

Will you pray with us as we begin our journey?

Dear loving, heavenly Father, I thank You that You care about me and the things going on in my life—the "big" things and the "little" things. Thank You that You care enough to show me what Your will is for me. I want to be led by Your Holy Spirit alone and to recognize Satan's deception when it comes. I believe that Your Word, the Bible, is the only ultimate source of truth. I commit myself in the power of Your Spirit to study it and learn what it says so that I may walk with You by faith. In Jesus' name, amen.

Let's Start at the Beginning

At a Christian retreat, a young man came up to me and asked, "Rich, how can I be sure that this girl I'm dating is the right one for me? How can I know if she is the one God wants me to marry?"

Another student approached me with a case of "senior panic"—he realized that it was time to make a decision about college. "I can't decide between a Christian college and a secular university, Rich. What do you think I should do?"

To date or not to date. To get a job or play a sport. To go on to college or try to make it in the business world. To go into the ministry or into a secular line of work. These are all great questions, and incredibly important ones.

Since you'll never find a verse in the Bible that says,

"Thou shalt marry thy girlfriend, Bubbles" or "My will, it's true, is found at State U.," how in the world can we know what God wants?

The answers to these and a thousand other questions like them really hinge on a much larger issue: Does God really love *me* enough to show me His will?

We have found that many young people today cannot solidly answer this crucial question, and so they flounder in a stormy sea of confusion. At one moment they are convinced of God's love and guidance, and then something happens to throw them for a loop—back into doubt and uncertainty.

Usually what happens next is that the young person goes to his or her youth pastor or trusted Christian friend to find "the answer."

Is that the only way we can discover God's will for us? We don't think so. You can personally become sensitive to God's love and leading and learn how to discern His will. This book will help you do just that.

God has given each of us His Word, which the Holy Spirit will use to open our eyes to what God's will is for us in most areas. But we must learn to take the time to wait on God and meditate on the truth of His Word in order to receive this kind of guidance. Most of us are too impatient for this. We want immediate answers. You know, flip open the Bible, point your finger at a verse, and expect our "vending machine God" to show us what we want to know.

It should not surprise us to find that God does not typically work that way.

God expects us to know the truth and to choose to walk by faith according to the truth of His Word. And this requires a disciplined study of the Bible.

In addition, every believer in Christ has the opportunity to personally be led by God's Spirit (as we will discuss in a later chapter) in matters not specifically covered by God's

Word. Again, however, we must latch onto and cling to one crucial truth in order to discern God's guidance: He unfailingly loves us. And that means He will gladly guide us.

His Word makes this truth crystal clear: "Yet I am always with you [God]; you hold me by my right hand. / You guide me with your counsel, and afterward you will take me into glory" (Ps. 73:23-24). King David found his God a constant source of guidance. And you can too.

Let me illustrate. Do I (Rich) love my daughter, Michelle? You bet I do. When she was three years old, we would have the greatest time taking walks together. I wanted her to see the amazing things in God's creation that she might miss on her own. Whether it was beautiful flowers that we picked together for her mommy or fire-ant hills that I kicked open to show her what was inside, we were both delighted with our times together.

But when we walked, I held her hand. Why? Because there were rocks to stumble over and muddy areas where she could slip. There were also cars that could harm her should she stray from my hand into the street. Plus it was just plain fun to hold hands with her!

Do I love Michelle enough to direct and guide her? Do I care enough to protect her and show her my longings for her? You'd better believe it! Well, if I am able to do so with such great love and delight, how much more is the God who *is* love able to do so?

You see, God's *will* for us is always revealed to us in the context of God's *love relationship* with us. And we'll never be able to trust God to show us His will if we do not once and for all drive a stake through the heart of our doubt about His love. Consider these verses from the Bible:

You see, at just the right time, when we were still powerless, Christ died for the ungodly. Very rarely will anyone die for a righteous man, though for a good man someone might pos-

sibly dare to die. But God demonstrates his own love for us in this: While we were still sinners, Christ died for us. (Rom. 5:6-8)

The cross of Christ ends the debate. Any doubts about God's love for you and me that may have been haunting us need to be laid to rest at the foot of Calvary's cross. Why? Because Jesus paid the ultimate sacrifice to show us once and for all that He (God) loves us.

The Disciples Doubted Too _____

His disciples showed the same doubt and panic we sometimes feel. They were in a boat crossing the Sea of Galilee when a terrible storm came up. Terrified, they woke Jesus, who was sleeping in the back of the boat. They cried out, "Teacher, don't you care if we drown?" (Mark 4:38).

Jesus quickly stilled the storm and then asked the disciples two questions that cut to the heart of the matter:

Why are you so afraid? Do you still have no faith?

Is that how you feel today? Are you filled with fear and doubt because you are uncertain that God loves *you* enough to still the storms in your life and guide you safely into His will on the other "shore"?

The disciples were afraid because Jesus was asleep. But as long as He was in the boat with them, these men really had nothing to fear. The same is true for you if you are a Christian. As long as Jesus is in your life, He's not going to let you sink. Learn to trust His love and power, even when it *seems* like He is asleep!

Are you worried that your concerns are too trivial for Him? Have you mistakenly thought that God wants you to "grow up" and rely on yourself now instead of Him? Nothing could be farther from the truth. Growth in Christ means a deepening dependence on Him, not a diminishing one.

On Thanksgiving I (Rich) was at a family reunion, and I overheard a conversation between a little girl and some adults. The girl had lost her ring while playing outside in the leaves and was very upset. The ring had been a gift from her mother.

Sensing the Spirit's tugging at my heart to help, I offered my great detective services. Ace Miller, Ring Detective, to the rescue!

On our walk to the area where she had lost it, I suggested to the girl that we pray, since God knew where the ring was and we didn't. In complete confidence I prayed, "Lord, would You please show us where to find this ring? In Jesus' name, amen."

I was excited that this eight-year-old would have the chance to see God's tender love for her demonstrated right before her eyes. I asked her to reenact her hand motions when the ring had flown off her finger. She did and we began searching in the general area. Ten minutes passed. Fifteen minutes. Nothing. I silently prayed, "Lord, please show us where the ring is. She needs to know You love her."

Twenty minutes. Thirty minutes went by. Still nothing. *Lord, don't You care about this little girl's ring? It means so much to her! Come on, Lord,* I urged silently. I have to admit that I was feeling anger and even some doubt by that time. Did God really care enough to show us where to look?

Suddenly an old man drove up. "Lose somethin'?" he asked.

"Yeah," I grumbled without looking up, "her ring." I pointed at the girl.

"Can I help?" the man asked.

Inside I was thinking, *Great, Lord. You send me an old man who can probably barely see. He's probably got one* foot in the grave and the other on a banana peel. That's just wonderful!

"Okay," I muttered.

And then God blew me away. The man walked around to the back of his car, unlocked his trunk, and pulled out a metal detector! Now, I don't know about where you live, but in Georgia people don't generally drive around with metal detectors in their trunks.

Five minutes later we found the ring, the little girl was elated, God was glorified, and I was humbled.

Later I reflected on what had happened. I kind of "congratulated" God on how He came through. I said to Him, "Lord, You're all right. That little girl needed to know that You care enough to handle even such a small thing as a lost ring."

The impression from God on my mind was unmistakable: "No, Rich, *you* needed to know that I care enough." And so I did. And I'll bet, so do you.

We suspect that you have some stories like this one, where God showed you in some unmistakable way how He cares for you. Can you conclude with us, then, that based on Jesus' death on the cross two thousand years ago, other biblical accounts, and God's work in your life today that He does truly love you? If so, then we're ready to tackle the next question: Can I really know His will for me?

Please pray with us:

Dear heavenly Father, thank You for proving Your love for me by sending Jesus to die for me. Thank You for the ways You've worked specifically in my life to confirm that love. As I seek to learn the ways You reveal Your will in my life, help me to stand on that unchanging love as a sure foundation. Help me to be confident that You will keep me on Your path through the Holy Spirit. In Jesus' name, amen.

PART 1

COUNTERFEIT GUIDANCE

Looking for Truth in All the Wrong Places

While sharing with a college group, I (Neil) could sense that one of the local heroes wasn't buying what I was saying. Rather than ignoring him, since he was distracting the group, I asked what he believed. He said, "I believe in this," putting his arm around his girlfriend. "I only believe in what I can see, feel, hear, and touch."

I asked him if he had a brain.

"You better believe it," he responded.

"Have you ever seen it, felt it, heard it, or touched it?" I asked.

"I know it's there because I can sense its effect," he said with confidence.

I said, "Look around, and you will see the effect of God's hand everywhere."

Then, a timid soul from another corner of the room entered into our discussion. "I think it's silly to argue about what is true," he began. "I believe in all religions. I just close my eyes and God reveals Himself to me. We can all be one with God if we will just let our minds be enlightened."

It was the same classroom, but there were completely opposite ways of looking at God and the world. The first boy's "scientific" view is called *western rationalism*. The second boy's "tune-in and turn-on" view is called *eastern mysticism*. And both ways of looking at life are nowhere near God's way.

Many teenagers today have bought into one or the other of these errors. How has that happened? How have we as a nation moved so far away from a biblical way of looking at things? It should not surprise us to see the slimy hand of Satan, the god of the world, behind this shift away from a God-centered life. From the beginning of time the devil has been trying to convince people that they don't really need God.

The Western Approach

One of Satan's more popular philosophies is called *secular humanism*. The *secular* part of that term has to do with the things of this world as opposed to the things of God. The *humanism* part has to do with man believing that he is capable of mastering his own destiny without God.

The philosophy of secular humanism throws off all the chains of superstition and religion and promotes the idea that man, by himself, is capable of living a fulfilling and good life. There's one big problem with that way of thinking, however. *It's wrong!*

This is the big lie the devil got Adam and Eve to swallow in the Garden of Eden. "You shall be like God!" Satan lied. And you know what happened when they bit into that deception: A whole Pandora's box of evil, sickness, and death came upon the world.

You see, without God as the "North Star" of our navigation through life, we drift endlessly and helplessly in an ocean of meaninglessness and despair. If we humans are only the chance result of millions of years of chemical reactions (evolution) and are not created in the image of a living, loving God, what hope do we have?

How did this idea of an "unnecessary God" show up in our society anyway? Well, as through science we made huge advances in knowledge and technology, we began to put our hope in science rather than in God to save us. We fell in love with the things our own hands could make and lost our deep sense of needing God.

And you can see how that happened: As we discovered cures for diseases, a means of exploring outer space, and ways to communicate globally, we became overwhelmingly impressed with our own abilities. And what *would* we do without the wonderful benefits of cars, telephones, medicine, computers, and TV (well, four out of five ain't bad!)?

Our lives have been profoundly changed and improved by scientific innovations, so it is not surprising to find that many people have come to believe that science is the "way, the truth, and the life."

Relying strictly on observation to discover truth is called *empiricism*. This philosophy says that by observation in a controlled environment, you can find out all you need to know. You simply analyze your data and come to rational conclusions.

But is that true in all cases? For example, can you scrutinize and analyze *love* under a microscope? Uh-uh. Believe it or not, some people believe love is just a function of chemicals and neurons in the brain! How romantic!

You see, what may work wonderfully for analyzing or predicting the behavior of hydrogen and oxygen molecules in a test tube fails miserably when it comes to matters of the human heart.

Why is that? Well, the scientific or empirical method was developed from the natural sciences (like chemistry and physics). There are indeed precise laws (which God created) that determine how atoms and molecules interact during controlled experiments. But the social sciences (like sociology and psychology), which examine human actions and reactions, are not nearly as precise.

Is it possible, for example, to predict based simply on observation and analysis how a person will react if he or she is subjected to physical or sexual abuse? No, it isn't.

Beyond that, is the idea of God as a loving Creator something we can prove or predict in a laboratory? He has revealed a lot of Himself in His Word, but He is far from scientifically explainable or predictable. He is the King who is sitting on His throne. He does whatever pleases Him. He acts and rules on His own authority.

Our adversary, the devil, is also unpredictable and difficult to study. And Jesus told us he is a liar and the father of lies. Even if he did decide to be interviewed by Barbara Walters, you couldn't believe a word he said. He is a deceiver by nature.

The spiritual world cannot be explored simply by observation and experimentation. We are not saying that the scientific method is *wrong*; we are saying it is *inadequate* to explain all of life in this world and beyond. We need a spiritual perspective.

A big problem with trying to draw conclusions without God's help is our lack of objectivity. We have all been influenced by our family, culture, education, and personal experience to the point that we are unable to be totally objective. We look at life through a filter, colored by our own knowledge (or ignorance!) and experience.

True knowledge and wisdom, however, require having a

relationship with God and the ability to see things from His perspective. "The fear of the LORD is the beginning of knowledge . . . [and] wisdom" (Prov. 1:7, 9:10).

Science is the study of the natural world that God created. This is good and necessary. But we need to interpret all *research* in the pure light of God's *revelation*—not the other way around. Our accurate research can show us what is. God's revelation of truth (the Bible) tells us *why* it is, what it should be, and what it will become.

The thing is, no matter how much we pride ourselves on being smart or right, our ability to think and draw conclusions is severely limited by three things:

1. We can never be sure we have all the necessary facts.
2. We can never be sure we are correctly interpreting the facts, because we cannot escape our own personal biases.
3. We can never be sure (without God's revelation) what the results will be of any course of action we choose.

Therefore, we desperately need God's guidance. God alone knows everything. God alone can decide with perfect wisdom, free from any corrupting influences—we can't. God *alone* knows the benefits or consequences of any action we decide to take.

Isaiah penned these words as God revealed to him a truth we all need to remind ourselves of every day:

"For my [God's] thoughts are not your thoughts, neither are your ways my ways," declares the LORD. "As the heavens are higher than the earth, so are my ways higher than your ways and my thoughts than your thoughts." (Isa. 55:8-9)

That may be humbling to admit, but it's also very freeing.

No longer are we forced to live by our wits alone, nor do we have to try to guess what God wants; we can know. How? By becoming more and more dependent on God and allowing Him to guide us by the Holy Spirit and the Word! He delights in revealing Himself and His will to those who strip off their pride and admit they need Him, as the apostle Paul wrote:

> *Where is the wise man? Where is the scribe? Where is the debater of this age? Has not God made foolish the wisdom of the world? For since in the wisdom of God the world through its wisdom did not come to know God, God was well-pleased through the foolishness of the message preached to save those who believe. (1 Cor. 1:20-21 NASB)*

An Eastern Approach

If you lived in India or China, chances are you would have grown up with a completely different approach to life than we do here in the West. The religions of Hinduism, Buddhism, and Taoism look for truth to come more by intuition, feeling, and impression than by science and reason.

In fact, supporters of eastern mysticism view the mind as the main hindrance to spiritual enlightenment. According to this philosophy, the mind must be bypassed in order for truth to be known. Here's an example from the teaching of Guru Maharaj-Ji:

> Ignorance is only created by the mind, and the mind keeps the secret that you are something divine away from you. This is why you have to tame the mind first. The mind is a snake, and the treasure is behind it. The snake lies over the treasure, so if you want that treasure, you will have to kill the snake. And killing the snake is not an easy job.[1]

You might say that eastern mystics are trying to "go out of their minds." And as you can gather from the Guru, some have succeeded in doing just that!

The first step toward spiritual insight, they say, is to ignore everything your mind is trying to tell you. Once you've done that (through yoga or meditation techniques), you can begin to tap into the "universal mind." The problem is that you are far more likely to tap into the god of this world (Satan) than you are the God of the Bible. You see, God works through your mind, while the devil tries to detour around it.

Everything from Transcendental Meditation (TM) to Silva Mind Control have flooded the American market—with great financial success. Most Americans, however, feel really nervous about slamming their brains into neutral. They are afraid of losing too much control. And so, enter the New Age movement with its only "half mindless" approach.

America's Religion of the Day _____

According to New Agers, the mind is the part of us that needs to achieve "cosmic consciousness." The mind needs to realize its oneness with the supreme, creative power of the universe, or so say the promoters of "science of mind" teaching.

Science of the mind is kind of like Grape Nuts cereal—you know, that crunchy stuff that is neither grapes nor nuts. Science of the mind is neither *scientific* nor should you pay it any *mind!* While New Agers say we create our own world around us by what we think, they are greatly mistaken. Only God can do that.

The New Age movement, then, is an incorrect way of understanding reality. It appeals to people who are fed up with organized religion—people who want the freedom to pick and choose what they believe, feel, and do. There are no strings attached to the New Ager. He can continue to sleep around, make all the money his greedy little heart desires, and do whatever else he chooses, and nobody is going to tell him he's wrong.

Appealing, huh? Sure—until the day he realizes that the strings that once held him to God and morality have been replaced by chains . . . to the god of this world. He's chosen his own destiny, all right, and it's full of destruction.

What are some of the main things that New Agers have in common? The first is *monism*—the belief that all is one and one is all. It is the Three Musketeers approach to religion. It says we all swim in one gigantic cosmic ocean (like a bunch of drips, I guess!). Supposedly all of mankind's problems come from failing to see ourselves as part of a single, united force.

According to monism, sin is not man's rebellion against God but rather man's fall into ignorance. Therefore, receiving salvation is not being restored to spiritual life by the grace of God, but coming to enlightenment about our cosmic oneness.

Satan tries to counterfeit everything that God does, and monism is his attempt at counterfeit unity, which Jesus defined in John 17:21. True unity is only possible as people are united together in Christ, walking in the light of God's truth and loving each other by the power of the Holy Spirit.

A second common belief of New Agers is *pantheism*—the belief that all is God. It comes naturally from believing that since all is one (including God), then all must be God. Why someone never concluded that since all is one (including slugs), then all must be slugs, I'll never know.

According to this belief, "God" becomes an impersonal force (à la *Star Wars*) that pervades all creation (trees, roaches, people—you name it). God is more of an "it" than a "He."

The third common thread among New Age believers is a *change in consciousness*. (To what? *Un*consciousness?) This is the obvious next step. If all is one and all is God, then I am God, right?

And once I come to this great revelation, I have had a change in my consciousness, which is referred to as "at-one-ment" (a counterfeit *atonement)*, self-realization, god-realization, enlightenment, or attunement.

The term *born again* is sometimes used by New Agers to describe this experience of realizing one's "godlikeness." This is a counterfeit conversion. Jesus used the term *born again* to describe the spiritual birth that takes place by the work of the Holy Spirit when a person puts his or her faith in the saving work of Christ. In reality, truly being "born again" involves coming to the realization that you are *not* God and Jesus is!

The fourth main factor that ties New Agers together is a *cosmic evolutionary optimism.* You might be saying now, "Say what?" Well, simply put, New Agers believe that the New Age (of Aquarius) is dawning in which the world will all come together under one world government.

Can you imagine billions of people, *all thinking they are God,* uniting? No way! Can you imagine the arguments over who's *really* in charge? That wouldn't be heaven; that would be hell!

The Bible tells us that one day Jesus Christ will come and rule the nations with a rod of iron (Rev. 2:27 NKJV). New Agers hope for a kingdom that is, in reality, a counterfeit kingdom—a kingdom of slavery to the prince of darkness.

The New Agers' fifth belief is that they can *create their own reality.* They are convinced they can determine reality by what they believe, so by changing what they believe, they can change their lives and world. For example, a New Ager might believe he or she could get into a particular college just by visualizing it happening in their mind.

Under this system, good and evil cease to be defined by an absolute standard like the Bible. Good and evil simply become what the New Ager decides they should be. Can you see the total chaos in society if the majority of people lived this way? It would be impossible to enforce laws because people couldn't agree on what crime is. It is downright chilling to think about!

The sixth and final area that unites New Agers (though they are generally unaware of this one) is that they *make contact with the kingdom of darkness*.

Though New Agers change the term *medium* to *channeler* and *demon* to *spirit guide*, the source of power they're accessing is satanic. As New Agers consult channelers and spirit guides for counsel and knowledge, they are like blind mice that have strolled right into the lair of the cat, unaware of the deadly threat right in front of them.

Recently I (Neil) received a call from a lady who was concerned about the turn of events in a small group she was attending. The group had started out innocently enough and was attended by supposedly Christian women. However, a woman in the group began to function as a medium, delivering messages from the spiritual realm. The women thought they were hearing from God.

They recorded six hours of videotape and transcribed the meetings into almost a hundred pages. During those six hours, the medium displayed five personalities. The group was convinced they were hearing from God, Jesus, the Holy Spirit, and two angels.

The woman who functioned as a medium was later identified as a non-Christian. There was a lot of evidence of this in the medium's actions. In the tape her eyes roll back as she falls into a trancelike state—which should have been a warning sign to the group. And at one point a voice says through her, "It's going to snow here tomorrow." I'm surprised that when it didn't snow the next day, the group couldn't see the snow job being done on them!

Help!

So where does the truth lie? Somewhere between the extremes of western rationalism and eastern mysticism. Jesus stated point blank, "I am . . . the truth" (John 14:6). God has chosen to reveal truth to us by direct revelation (the Bible). As we expose ourselves to God's Word, He fills our minds with the truth and our hearts with love and joy.

Our world desperately needs truth, love, and joy. The Bible tells us that we can know *all things,* yet we're *nothing* without love (1 Cor. 13:2). Scripture teaches that "knowledge puffs up, but love builds up" (1 Cor. 8:1). Which does the world need more?

Until recently I (Rich) was driven by the need to be right. Winning mattered more to me than how I treated my opponents.

Then one day God spoke to me powerfully through the last verse in 1 Corinthians 13. It says, "And now these three remain: faith, hope and love. But the greatest of these is love." God showed me that I was not living as if love was the greatest. I was filled with a tremendous amount of knowledge, ambition, and drive, but along the way, I hurt the people who disagreed with me.

I am now asking the Lord to make me a people-lover. I want to serve other people, not my own desire. And by His grace, He is beginning that process. You see, people really don't care how much you know until they know how much you care.

Knowledge is never meant to be an end in itself. If all our *right thinking* doesn't lead us to *radical loving* of God and people, we are indeed nothing.

The balance is clear in Scripture. It is the truth that sets us free (John 8:32), but truth is not simply an idea but a person—Jesus. Jesus explained that if the *Son* would make us free, we would be free indeed (John 8:36). And freedom starts when we submit our *minds* to the truth.

Any desire or plan to find out the will of God must begin and end with Jesus Christ. There are no shortcuts or detours around Him. *He is the way.* Jesus is the ultimate revelation of God, the very Word of God. *He is the truth.* All attempts to find meaning, happiness, significance, or satisfaction in our lives without Jesus lead only to dead ends. *He is the life.*

We must come to know, believe, and live according to these wise words of that wisest of men, Solomon: "Trust in the LORD with all your heart and lean not on your own understanding; in all your ways acknowledge him, and he will make your paths straight" (Prov. 3:5-6).

When we receive Christ by faith, we are all whisked away forever from the domain of darkness and ushered into the kingdom of light. However, though we are all in Christ, we are not all the same.

Some Christians strive to be right and search for only wisdom and knowledge. Others seek for reality and power and operate more emotionally. Both are needed in your youth group and in your church.

The Bible says we need to live in harmony with one another (1 Peter 3:8). In music, different notes blended together produce a far more beautiful sound than one note alone. The same is true in relationships. If we can grow to love and appreciate each other and seek to learn from one another, we will begin to see a fuller expression of the beauty and power of God!

Do you want to know the will of God? Then ask Him to produce in you the balance that only He can create. Right *and* real. Loving *and* wise. Zealous *and* full of knowledge. Clear-minded *and* compassionate. That is God's will and desire for you. If it is also your desire for you, will you join us in praying?

Dear heavenly Father, Your ways and thoughts are so much higher than mine that I can never know You and Your will apart from Your revealing Yourself to me. More than anything else, that's what I long for. I choose today to stop trying to figure out who You are and what You want for me on my own. I choose to trust in You with all my heart and not lean on my own ability to think or guess or feel or imagine. Thank You for Your Word, which is truth, and which the Holy Spirit will use to lead me to the Truth, the Lord Jesus. May You use me to touch the lives of those around me who are trapped in the lies of the devil. I choose to walk with You now as my Lord. Amen.

CHAPTER 3

The Devil Hates You and Has a Terrible Plan for Your Life

During the last year I (Rich) have had the joy of getting to know John. John revealed to me that as a young boy, he had gone to sleep every night for almost five years listening to a spooky radio show. During that time he started "hearing" a voice in his head that told him ahead of time when the phone would ring and who would be calling! Understandably, John thought that was pretty cool. As time went on, the voice in his mind grew stronger, often giving him helpful advice before he left the house.

Because most of the time what the voice told him was good, John came to think that this was God speaking to him. But at times the voice also made him feel worthless and useless. And so John came to believe that was how God felt about him.

As the voice continued to express "God's rejection" to

John, he became so gripped with fear, insecurity, and anger that he could no longer function. He eventually recognized that "the voice of God" on which he had relied for so long was in reality a spirit guide (demon) pretending to be the Holy Spirit.

As a result of going through *The Steps to Freedom in Christ* John, with great difficulty at first, was able to tell the spirit guide to beat it. Today, John is a free man, no longer plagued by the fear, self-doubt, and intense anger that ruled his life. John had fallen prey to a deceiving spirit.

We would all do well to listen to the warning of the apostle John: "Dear friends, do not believe every spirit, but test the spirits to see whether they are from God" (1 John 4:1).

That great saint and founder of the Methodist Church, John Wesley, echoed the apostle John's words when he wrote:

> Do not hastily ascribe things to God. Do not easily suppose dreams, voices, impressions, visions or revelations to be from God. They may be from Him. They may be from nature. They may be from the devil. Therefore, do not believe every spirit, but try [test] the spirits, whether they be from God.[1]

Does God really give us personal guidance? Absolutely. Can deceiving spirits give us false guidance as well? Yes, they can. Even to Christians? Yes. And here is the problem: Satan counterfeits the way the Lord leads by giving us false impressions, trying to convince us that we are hearing the voice of God in our minds. And that is exactly where the battle is going on for control of our lives . . . *in our minds*.

This was clearly revealed by the research done for the book, *The Seduction of Our Children*. Steve Russo and I (Neil) surveyed over 1,700 professing Christian junior and senior high students. In that survey:

- Forty-eight percent said they have experienced some presence (seen or heard) in their room that scared them. (And we're not talking about their little brother or sister!)
- Fifty percent said they have had bad thoughts about God.
- About one-third said that it is hard for them to concentrate while praying and reading the Bible.
- Around two-thirds have heard voices in their head, like there was a subconscious self talking to them.
- Nearly one out of five said they frequently had thoughts of suicide.
- Over 20 percent have had impulsive thoughts to kill somebody.[2]

These statistics may shock you. Then again, they may enable you to breathe a sigh of relief, knowing that you are not alone.

As we share the truth with people who are experiencing these kinds of battles for their minds, they are relieved to know that they are *not* going crazy. They are under spiritual attack. And you can defeat the devil in the battle for your mind, because Christ has already won the war!

You see, if you went to the average non-Christian psychiatrist and told him you were hearing voices, he or she would probably think you were hallucinating. The diagnosis would likely be that you were a paranoid schizophrenic or psychotic, and the treatment would probably be drugs.

Now, do we believe that two-thirds of the Christian teenagers in our survey are mentally ill? No, we don't! Instead, we believe 1 Timothy 4:1, which says, "The Spirit clearly says that in later times some will abandon the faith and follow deceiving spirits and things taught by demons."

So who is really out of touch with reality—the Christian teenager who is under attack by deceiving spirits or the psychiatrist who doesn't believe in the demonic world at all? We'll let you and the Bible answer that one.

The most important factors in being a mentally healthy young person are having a true picture of who God is and who you are as a child of God. If either or both of these things are distorted, you will have struggles.

Are those struggles spiritual, mental, or emotional? All of the above. God is always present and deeply involved in our lives, and at the same time, the devil is constantly trying to tempt, accuse, and deceive us. So our problems are always spiritual. And these spiritual problems show themselves through the way we think and believe (mental) and how we feel (emotional).

Unfortunately many Christians are so ignorant of the devil's schemes (like my friend John at the beginning of this chapter) that they are paying attention to deceiving spirits instead of the Spirit of truth. We desperately need to know how Satan operates so that we can defend ourselves.

Satan's Strategies _____

Let's talk about *temptation*. Our flesh (that part of us that still wants to do its own thing, not God's) is easily tempted. The devil uses the things in the world around us to tempt our flesh. How? Every temptation of Satan is an attempt to get us to meet our real needs on our own and apart from God.

God promises to "meet all your needs according to his glorious riches in Christ Jesus" (Phil. 4:19). We get into trouble when we look to anything other than the Lord to take care of us. In my (Neil) book *Living Free in Christ,* I show how the most important needs of our lives are met in Christ.

Satan also constantly engages in *accusation*. Have you ever had your mind filled with thoughts like *I'm a jerk, I can't do anything right, God doesn't love me,* or *I can't live the Christian life?* The devil wants us to believe that we are less than God says we are. If you believe his taunts, you will live a defeated life.

Notice that Satan is able to make the thoughts seem like they are coming from you (e.g., *I'm a nerd*). Over time, if you believe them, they *will* become your thoughts, but the initial impression is from the devil. These kinds of thoughts are never ever from God, who says:

> *But you are a chosen people, a royal priesthood, a holy nation, a people belonging to God, that you may declare the praises of him who called you out of darkness into his wonderful light. Once you were not a people, but now you are the people of God; once you had not received mercy, but now you have received mercy. (1 Peter 2:9-10)*

Satan's trickiest tactic, however, is neither temptation nor accusation. You see, when you are being tempted, you know it. If you are being accused, you know that too. But if you are being deceived, you don't know it. That is the nature of the devil's number-one strategy, *deception.*

The Bible reveals the reason for Satan's deception in 2 Corinthians 11:3: "But I am afraid that just as Eve was deceived by the serpent's cunning, your minds may somehow be led astray from your sincere and pure devotion to Christ."

The devil is a liar (John 8:44), and he is constantly seeking to lead our minds astray from the truth. Why? Because he does not want us to be sincerely and purely devoted to Jesus. If he can get us to shift away from the truth of the Bible and our close relationship with Jesus, Satan knows that in time we will grow weak in faith. We will become unable to discern the guidance of God and then the devil will be able to lure us away from the will of God. The result? Bondage. Being trapped by the devil to do *his* will.

That's why you need to know the truth, because "the truth will set you free" (John 8:32). You need to walk with Jesus, because He is "the way and the truth and the life" (John 14:6). You need to be filled with the Holy Spirit who is the "Spirit of truth," who will "guide you into all truth" (John 16:13).

When you put on the armor of God, the first thing you do is "stand firm . . . with the belt of truth buckled around your waist" (Eph. 6:14). So buckle up with God's safety belt of truth! It's not just a good idea, it's God's will!

Don't Believe Everything You Hear ___

If Satan can creep undetected into your life, family, or youth group and get you (or y'all) to believe a lie, he can control you. Don't let him. Become an expert in the truth of God's Word. Then you'll be able to "demolish arguments and every pretension that sets itself up against the knowledge of God, and . . . take captive every thought to make it obedient to Christ" (2 Cor. 10:4-5).

I (Rich) was once at a conference where Neil was speaking. Seated next to me was a friend of my family. After Neil's message on "The Battle for the Mind," she suddenly said, "That's a lie!"

"What's a lie? What are you hearing in your head?" I asked.

"I just had a thought. It said, 'God is going to touch everyone's life in this auditorium except yours.'"

"Boy, what a lie that is," I replied. "God loves you as much as He loves me or anyone else here."

By simply sharing that deceiving thought and renouncing (rejecting) it out loud, Julie (not her real name) gained power over the enemy's deception. As we talked further, we came to see that the devil had been lying to her in this way for years.

Julie had no problem believing that God would use her to touch others. She had real problems, however, believing God loved her enough to personally touch her life. Now she knows the love of God in her *heart* and not just in her *head,* and she is experiencing His love daily.

Deception can happen to the most godly and sincere believers. But the power of the truth of God will smash the enemy's chains. Just ask Julie.

A Deadly Cancer

Perhaps the greatest access that Satan has to the minds of believers today is in the area of bitterness and unforgiveness. Read carefully the words of the apostle Paul, inspired by the Holy Spirit: "'In your anger do not sin': Do not let the sun go down while you are still angry, and do not give the devil a foothold" (Eph. 4:26-27).

It is a normal reaction to pain, rejection, and humiliation to feel anger. That knee-jerk reflex emotion of getting mad is not sin. Sin happens when we let that anger smolder inside us. Rather than letting it go, we nurse the grudge and it continues to fester. Anger becomes resentment. Resentment becomes bitterness and unforgiveness. And unforgiveness may lead to revenge.

Jesus told us that we need to forgive from the heart or we will be tormented (Matt. 18:34-35). And anyone who has harbored bitterness in their heart knows the reality of that torment, for bitterness is like a horrible cancer in our bodies. If we don't forgive, it will eventually eat us alive from the inside out.

I (Rich) was talking to a teenage girl about her relationship with her dad, who had deserted the family when she was two. Her face became hard, angry, and bitter.

"You hate your dad, don't you?" I asked gently. I might as well have been talking to the Rock of Gibraltar. She was as hard as stone.

I continued, "You're going to have to let go of your anger toward your dad and forgive him, Cheri [not her real name], if you want to be free. There's no other way."

And what I said is absolutely true. For some, forgiving others is just a small hill to climb. No blood, sweat, or tears. For others, it feels like climbing Mt. Everest, especially if there has been severe abuse. Although there are no shortcuts or tunnels through this mountain, God promises to graciously walk with us all the way to the top and over to the other side . . . where freedom is.

Cheri was not willing to forgive her dad that day. And so she walked away still locked in the bondage of her bitterness.

One year later I saw her again. Her face was radiant with joy and love. The granite grimace was gone.

"You finally forgave your dad, didn't you, Cheri?" I asked, smiling.

She nodded and smiled back.

"And now you're free. Praise God!"

It is your responsibility and mine to use our minds, reject the lies and deceptions of the enemy, and choose to walk in the truth. No one can make those decisions for us. Consider these Scriptures that emphasize our need to keep from passively shifting our minds into neutral and to actively choose the truth:

- Do not think of yourself more highly than you ought, but rather think of yourself with sober judgment. (Rom. 12:3)
- Brothers, stop thinking like children. In regard to evil be infants, but in your thinking be adults. (1 Cor. 14:20)

- Therefore, prepare your minds for action; be self-controlled; set your hope fully on the grace to be given you when Jesus Christ is revealed. (1 Peter 1:13)
- Finally, brothers, whatever is true, whatever is noble, whatever is right, whatever is pure, whatever is lovely, whatever is admirable—if anything is excellent or praiseworthy—think about such things. (Phil. 4:8)

A lot of the questions you may have about God's will would be answered if you simply used Philippians 4:8 as a test. Do you desire to follow Christ and be obedient to His will enough to take your music, TV viewing, movies, video games, and reading material through the acid test of Philippians 4:8?

Would you pray right now and ask God to shine the light of Philippians 4:8 on your thought life, your daydreams, and your conversations with friends at school and on the phone?

As you learn to keep your mind on pure things, you'll be more alert to deceiving spirits. If a thought comes into your mind that seems questionable, take it right to Philippians 4:8 and ask the Lord to reveal to you if it is true, noble, right, pure, lovely, etc. Then follow what the next verse in Scripture tells you to do: "Whatever you have learned or received or heard from me, or seen in me—put it into practice. And the God of peace will be with you" (Phil. 4:9).

If we really desire to follow God, we will *know* the truth and we will *obey* the truth. Then we will find freedom from the control of deceiving spirits.

As we counsel teens and adults, we have two main desires: One, to help them know who they are as children of God. And two, to help them experience freedom and peace of mind.

With these desires I (Neil) tried to help a missionary who

was struggling to hold her life together. After our time together, she sent me this letter:

> The edge of tension and irritation is gone. I feel so free. The Bible has been really exciting, stimulating, and more understandable than ever before. I am no longer bound by accusations, doubts, thoughts of suicide, murder, or other harm that comes straight from hell into my head. There is a serenity in my mind and spirit, a clarity of consciousness that is profound. I've been set free. . . . Not only is my spirit more serene, my head is actually clearer. . . .
>
> My relationship with God has changed significantly. For eight years, I felt He was distant from me. . . . I wanted so badly to meet with Him, to know His presence again. I needed to know Him as a friend and companion, not as the distant authority figure He had become in my mind and experience. Now that I am free in Christ, I have seen my ability to trust grow and my ability to be honest with Him increase greatly. I really am experiencing the spiritual growth I had been praying for.

Who wouldn't want that kind of freedom, joy, and closeness to God? Isn't this your desire as well? Don't you want to put an end to Satan's deception in your mind and be freed from his attempts to control your life? If so, would you pray with us?

Dear heavenly Father, thank You that Jesus came to set the captives free. Since I have accepted Your free gift of salvation, I know that I am Your child, seated with Christ in heaven. I choose to believe the truth that nothing can ever separate me from Your love nor snatch me out of Your hand. Deep inside me, the Holy Spirit bears witness that I am Your child.
I realize that it is my responsibility to take every thought captive to the obedience of Christ. So I choose

to reject the lies of Satan and instead believe Your truth, Lord. I will not let my mind dwell on any music, thoughts, conversations, TV shows, video games, or anything else that does not stand up to the acid test of Philippians 4:8.

Please forgive me for the times I have given in to the temptations, accusations, and deceptions of the enemy. Forgive me for ever doubting Your great love for me. In the name of Christ I resist the evil one, and I choose to walk with Jesus. Amen.

CHAPTER 4

Prophecy Today: The Good, the Bad, and the Ugly

One afternoon I (Neil) was sitting in a coffee shop waiting for my son to finish soccer practice. A young man noticed I was reading my Bible and asked if I was studying to be a Christian. I told him I'd been a Christian for some time, and I asked him if he had ever made a decision for Christ. He said he had just become a Christian.

He told me that two friends had given a prophecy for him specifying what he should do with his life. He was troubled because the prophecies were not the same. "Which one should I believe?" he asked.

"Neither," I suggested. I asked if he believed that all Christians had a personal relationship with God. He said he wasn't sure what that meant, so I explained to him that all of God's children have access to Him. I said, "If God wanted you to do something, wouldn't He tell you?"

Prophecy is really "in" these days. Christians are enamored with the gift of prophecy, and many long to be known as prophets of God. These prophet-wanna-bes are all over the place, giving so-called "words from the Lord." Some even begin speaking by saying, "Thus saith the Lord. . . ." Many people are afraid to oppose them or what they say for fear they will be opposing God Himself. In your search for God's will for your life, choose carefully whom you listen to.

Certainly we do not want to try to put God in a box and say, "He never works like that," but we also need to be brave enough to ask the tough questions. For example: Are there prophets today? Is there still a gift of prophecy? What are the marks of a false prophet? How can you discern the voice of God from counterfeits?

There is no question that this is an important issue today. And there is no doubt that as we approach the time of Christ's return, it will become an even more critical one! Jesus Himself sternly warned His disciples:

> *At that time if anyone says to you, "Look, here is the Christ!" or, "There he is!" do not believe it. For false Christs and false prophets will appear and perform great signs and miracles to deceive even the elect [God's people]— if that were possible. See, I have told you ahead of time. (Matt. 24:23-25)*

> *Watch out that you are not deceived. For many will come in my name, claiming, "I am he," and, "The time is near." Do not follow them. (Luke 21:8)*

Jesus made it clear that in the latter days, deception would run rampant in the world, operating in the name of Christ and God. In order for us to walk in the truth and not be deceived, we need to look at what God's Word says about this whole matter of prophets and prophecy.

A Look at the Book

In the Old Testament, those who spoke for God were called *prophets*. Moses was a prophet, as were Isaiah, Jeremiah, Ezekiel, and many others. They did not simply decide one day to become God's spokesmen; they were called by God Himself. For example, the following is the account of God's call to Jeremiah:

> The word of the LORD came to me [Jeremiah], saying,
>
> > "Before I formed you in the womb I
> > knew you,
> > before you were born I set you
> > apart;
> > I appointed you as a prophet to the
> > nations."
>
> "Ah, Sovereign LORD," I said, "I do not know how to speak; I am only a child."
> But the LORD said to me, "Do not say, 'I am only a child.' You must go to everyone I send you to and say whatever I command you." (Jer. 1:4-7)

It was not a glamorous job to be called by God as His prophet. Jeremiah obviously was not too thrilled about being chosen. And no wonder—many of the prophets ended up getting beaten or killed for their preaching.

After the prophet Malachi, there was a four-hundred-year silence during which no prophet of God arose. Then came John the Baptist, who is usually considered the last of the Old Testament-style prophets. His job was to point people to the Word of God, and not simply the spoken Word, but the living Word, Jesus Christ. Jesus the Son is the ultimate Word from the Lord, as the writer of Hebrews makes clear:

In the past God spoke to our forefathers through the prophets at many times and in various ways, but in these last days he has spoken to us by his Son, whom he appointed heir of all things, and through whom he made the universe. (Heb. 1:1-2)

Does God still have prophets today? Most biblical scholars believe that the Bible is a finished product, and therefore the men who wrote the Bible—prophets (as in the Old Testament) and apostles (as in the New Testament)—are no longer necessary. Every believer in Christ now has an equal opportunity to know the Word and will of God through studying the Bible under the direction of the Holy Spirit.

Since the time the church pronounced the Bible complete, many false teachers and false prophets have shown up, claiming to have "new revelation" from God.

Joseph Smith (founder of the Mormons) claimed that truth equal in authority to the Bible can be found in other books, such as *The Book of Mormon.* Charles Taze Russell and other leaders of the cult called Jehovah's Witnesses have rewritten the Bible to make it fit their view of Christ, the judgment, hell, and other issues.

Islam, while holding various men of the Bible in high esteem (including Jesus), has concluded that the Bible is full of errors. Mohammed, they claim, is the last and greatest prophet of God and the Koran is the only true holy book.

If anyone comes along proclaiming "new truth" or a new "word from the Lord," warning bells should go off in your head and red lights flash before your eyes. God is *building* His church, that's true, but the foundation has already been laid by the apostles and prophets. Jesus Christ Himself is the chief cornerstone (Eph. 2:20).

God continues His work today by providing pastors/teachers and evangelists who teach and equip Christians to do the work of God in this world (Eph. 4:11-13). Their job is not to try and discover new things God has never said before. Their role is to take what God has already said (in the Bible) and, under the direction of the Holy Spirit, apply it to the ever-changing circumstances of life.

A Prophet of God . . . Not! _____

As we have said before, Satan tries to counterfeit the things of God. And since God used prophets in the Old Testament, it should not surprise us that the devil had his false prophets as well. How did God warn the people to recognize false ones? Deuteronomy 18:21-22 offers a very simple test for a prophet. If what he predicted never occured, that man had not been sent by God. And that makes sense! Since God knows the future perfectly, the one He would send to predict the future would obviously get it right.

The poor fool who made a prediction that failed would get stoned (and we're not talking about marijuana!). A 99 percent success rate was not even good enough (although that would far surpass the fortune-tellers of today!). It was 100 percent accurate or be rocked until you rolled over dead.

Believe it or not, however, the main role of a prophet in the Old Testament was not to predict the future. His chief purpose was to call people to repent of their sins and idols (false gods) and to return to the true God. Therefore, God needed to give another litmus test for the people to determine if a so-called prophet really came from God or not, and He did so in Deuteronomy 13:1-3:

If a prophet, or one who foretells by dreams, appears among you and announces to you a miraculous sign or wonder, and if the sign or wonder of which he has spoken takes place, and he says, "Let us follow other gods" (gods you have not known) "and let us worship them," you must not listen to the words of that prophet or dreamer. The LORD your God is testing you to find out whether you love him with all your heart and with all your soul.

Do you see how easy it would have been to be duped by one of these false prophets? They were flashy and impressive and powerful. They seemed able to perform dazzling things at times. In desperate times desperate people grabbed at any ray of hope.

Things have not changed much since then. People are still easily faked out by any kind of supernatural event (e.g., a shadow on a wall that looks like the face of Jesus or a statue of Mary that "cries"), because they mistakenly believe that everything "miraculous" must be from God.

Nothing could be farther from the truth. God warned us that it would be possible for false prophets to perform miraculous signs and wonders. But these impostors are rebellious at heart (Deut. 13:5) and they seek to lure people away from the true God to false gods (demons). The "miracles" are the bait, and the trap is that the devil wants people to look to these false gods for spiritual direction rather than to the living God.

Several years ago I (Neil) had a college ministry near Long Beach, California. A nearby ministry created quite a controversy. Everybody was hearing about the great miracles coming true at the hands of its young prophet. Several students under my ministry went to the Friday evening services, which were held in a rented theater. God seemed to be blessing that work far more than mine. Eventually, though, the "prophet" moved his ministry to another city, and a few years later he died of AIDS as a result of his immoral lifestyle. A lot of people, including those former students of mine, were led down the wrong path.

We need to wake up to the reality that false prophets and teachers performing wondrous signs will increase as the time of the Antichrist or lawless one draws near. All other cult leaders will look like Winnie-the-Pooh compared to him. He will be the most deceptive man who ever lived, as the New Testament clearly warns:

> *The coming of the lawless one will be in accordance with the work of Satan displayed in all kinds of counterfeit miracles, signs and wonders, and in every sort of evil that deceives those who are perishing. They perish because they refused to love the truth and so be saved. For this reason God sends them a powerful delusion so that they will believe the lie and so that all will be condemned who have not believed the truth but have delighted in wickedness. (2 Thess. 2:9-12)*

That's heavy stuff, we know, but God wants us to be forewarned. There is no need to be afraid, just on the alert. Don't get caught up in the hysteria or excitement of dreamers and prophets, even those that perform miracles. Get caught up in the joy of knowing and walking with Jesus Christ. And steer clear of anyone who does not humbly teach the truth of God's Word.

What about the gift of prophecy that the New Testament talks about in 1 Corinthians 14? Let's go straight to the source and see what its purpose is: "Everyone who prophesies speaks to men for their strengthening, encouragement and comfort. He who . . . prophesies edifies [builds up] the church" (1 Cor. 14:3-4).

The role of the gift of prophecy in the life of the church is to strengthen the hearts of the believers to return to God and walk with Him, no matter how tough things may be. But there is another role of the gift of prophecy, described later in that same chapter of Scripture by the apostle Paul:

> *If an unbeliever or someone who does not understand comes in while everybody is prophesying, he will be convinced by all that he is a sinner and will be judged by all, and the secrets of his heart will be laid bare. So he will fall down and worship God, exclaiming, "God is really among you!" (1 Cor. 14:24-25)*

God's Word is like a fire that purifies the church and like a hammer that breaks up the hard ground and softens peoples' hearts (Jer. 23:29). When those with the gift of prophesy are properly exercising their Spirit-led ministry, the people of God will be built up and the resistance of unbelievers will be broken down.

As we have already heard from Jesus, false prophets and teachers will be like a growing plague in the world. Aside from the ways already mentioned, how can we recognize them?

The first clue in sniffing out a false prophet is his (or her) unrighteous life. Let's tune in to Jesus' warning again:

> *Not everyone who says to me, "Lord, Lord," will enter the kingdom of heaven, but only he who does the will of my Father who is in heaven. Many will say to me on that day, "Lord, Lord, did we not prophesy in your name, and in your name drive out demons and perform many miracles?" Then I will tell them plainly, "I never knew you. Away from me, you evildoers!" (Matt. 7:21-23)*

A good chunk of the book of 2 Peter is written to unmask false prophets and teachers. Some or all of the following traits will be typical of the ones you may run into: greed, controlling behavior, and exaggeration (2 Peter 2:3), pride and a desire to be in the spotlight rather than truly glorifying (obeying) God (2 Peter 2:10), and sexual sin (2 Peter 2:13-14).

In addition, what they teach will not line up with the Word of God, though it may be hard to tell that at first (2 Peter 2:1). In the end, however, many people will fall for the fakes' show and as a result of their sinful behavior and corrupt teaching, the reputation of the true church of Jesus Christ will be hurt (2 Peter 2:2).

Another trait of false prophets and teachers is that they will often work from within the church. We are not to go around suspiciously accusing our church leaders just because we may not like them, but we are to recognize the real threat of Satan's human puppets infiltrating the church:

For such men are false apostles, deceitful workmen, masquerading as apostles of Christ. And no wonder, for Satan himself masquerades as an angel of light. It is not surprising, then, if his servants masquerade as servants of righteousness. Their end will be what their actions deserve. (2 Cor. 11:13-15)

These false teachers work secretly, disguised in the cloaks of clergy. They are like enemy agents that have crept behind our lines to sabotage the work of God. Believe it or not, some are hard-core Satanists who have been trained to destroy churches from within.

Always causing divisions and quarrels, these people are masters at getting the people of God to fight among themselves. And if Christians are busy battling one another, they have no time, energy, or desire to fight their real enemy, Satan!

Yet another trait of false prophets and teachers is their rebellious heart. They can't stand anyone in authority (2 Peter 2:10), and they won't listen to anyone but themselves.

They will do everything they can to ruin the reputation of church leaders while undermining everything the leaders try to do.

If they are able to worm their way into leadership themselves, they will use it as a power trip to promote their own ideas and ambitions. This is in direct contrast to the Lord Jesus, who "did not come to be served, but to serve" (Matt. 20:28).

While being alert to the reality of false prophets and teachers, don't go on a witch-hunt. Don't condemn someone just because you dislike their personality or their style of preaching or teaching. We are to *discern,* but not to judge. We need to be careful not to judge others lest we also be judged (Matt. 7:1-2). There are many sincere believers in Christ who are struggling with sin in their lives. They are not evil; they are in bondage. Our hearts and prayers need to go out to them.

Your responsibility as a young person is to "obey your leaders and submit to their authority. They keep watch over you as men who must give an account. Obey them so that their work will be a joy, not a burden, for that would be of no advantage to you" (Heb. 13:17).

Choose your leaders carefully, according to the wisdom and warnings offered in God's Word. Then pray and encourage them by submitting to their authority. If, however, what they teach consistently violates the truth of Scripture, you probably need to find a different church.

If your parents forbid such a move, pray that God will move in their hearts as you share your concerns gently with them. Do not make demands of them. Be patient. Seek out other avenues of good Christian teaching (such as books, tapes, radio) in addition to your own Bible study. Spend time with Christian friends on a regular basis. God will meet your spiritual needs, even if your parents don't see things your way.

The Big Five _____

Here are some Christian teachings that we feel must be in place for a church to be healthy. There are others, but these are the ones that are the most likely to be ignored or denied by false prophets and false teachers. We'll call these the Big Five, and if they are pillars of your church, you're probably in the right place!

1. Jesus Christ must be honored and worshiped as both Son of God and God the Son.
2. God must be understood to exist as one God eternally present in three distinct Persons: Father, Son, and Holy Spirit.
3. The crucifixion of Christ for the forgiveness of sins, the bodily resurrection of Jesus from the dead, and His bodily return (Second Coming) must be believed and taught.
4. The Bible must be held up as the only infallible Word of God and not viewed as only partially true or corrupted. No other book or teaching must be considered as even in the same league as the Bible.
5. The way of salvation must be clearly taught as totally by the grace of God through faith in Jesus Christ alone, with no "works" or "duties" added on as necessary for forgiveness of sin and eternal life.

The balance is found most clearly in 1 Thessalonians 5:19-22. Follow this instruction and you will not go wrong: "Do not put out the Spirit's fire; do not treat prophecies with contempt. Test everything. Hold on to the good. Avoid every kind of evil."

And know that God wants you to develop a deepening dependence on Him, not primarily on people, to know His will. He delights in you with a strong and affectionate love and He longs for you to know His love. And in the context of that love relationship, He will show you His path clearly. You can count on it. How do we know? He told us so: "I will instruct you and teach you in the way you should go; I will counsel you and watch over you" (Ps. 32:8).

With all the voices clamoring for our attention, and with Satan still using false prophets to deceive us, will you join us in prayer that we may know the truth God wants us to know . . . truth that will set us free and keep us free?

Dear loving, heavenly Father. More than anything I want to know You and Your will. I want to experience Your presence in my life and follow You alone. I don't want to follow any false teachers or prophets, nor do I want any counterfeit gifts.

Every spiritual ability I have, I bring before You. If it is not from You, then I renounce it and confess my sin of not being more discerning. Thank You for Your forgiveness. If what I have experienced in my life is from You, then I pray that You would give me the power and wisdom to use this gift for Your glory.

I want only You to be my Lord and so I commit myself to growing in my relationship with You. I choose to develop my faith in You by the joyful study of Your Word. Fill me with Your Holy Spirit so that I might have the ability to meet the needs of the hurting people around me. In Jesus' name, amen.

Looking
Fear
Straight
in the Eye

At a Bible study for families at our church, I (Rich) was talking to two teenage girls about Satan's strategy to intimidate and cause fear in believers.

"We have seen an evil presence in our room at night, and we're scared to death of it," one of them confessed.

Fear.

Another man, who had been the victim of incest since the time he was five years old, told a friend and me (Rich) that he was filled with fear and rarely went anywhere anymore. Psychologists would say he was agoraphobic, afraid to be out in public.

Fear.

It is quite common for people to speak of having "panic or anxiety attacks." This occurs when unexplained terror grabs people in a suffocating bear hug and won't let them go.

Fear.

Fear is one of the most powerful controllers around. Fear of the future and fear of death drive people to consult fortune-tellers and channelers.

Fear of rejection causes teens to compromise with the world and sin, keeping silent about their faith in Christ.

The fear of failure constantly nips at the heels of businessmen, athletes, students, and even ministers, compelling them to work harder and longer and better . . . until they get so stressed out, burned out, or wiped out that they have to drop out.

Does God want us to be controlled by the fear of people, Satan, death, or anything else? No way! The writer of Proverbs declares, "The wicked flee when no one is pursuing, / But the righteous are as bold as a lion" (Prov. 28:1 NASB).

The New Testament echoes those words when it says, "For God has not given us a spirit of fear, but of power and of love and of a sound mind" (2 Tim. 1:7 NKJV). God wants us to walk boldly by faith, not timidly in fear.

True, there is such a thing as a healthy fear. We ought to be afraid of getting hit by a car, for example, so we take appropriate steps. We don't play out in the traffic! Such fears are a part of normal, God-given common sense.

But fear that controls our lives and paralyzes our walk of faith in God is not from Him! It is like an alien transmission that drives out all "faith signals" and takes over the video screen of our mind. It broadcasts a message that robs us of strength, love, and clear thinking. It replaces them with weakness, self-centeredness, and confusion.

Unhealthy fear either compels us to do what is wrong, or it hinders us from doing what we know is right. It is nothing more than a bullying tactic straight from the biggest bully of them all, Satan.

Fear and *anxiety* are similar and yet different. People become anxious over something uncertain or unknown: *Will she say yes when I call her up for a date? Will I be able to make enough money to pay for college now that Dad is unemployed? Will I pass my driver's exam?* Stuff like that.

Fear, on the other hand, has a definite object. People are afraid of someone or something, like death, people, Satan, spiders, snakes, school cafeteria food. You get the idea.

Why are we afraid of certain things? First, the object is nearby. Second, the object of our fear is something we believe could harm us. Every fear object therefore must be something that we see as being both *present* and *powerful*.

For example, I (Rich) have watched enough *Jaws* movies and seen enough National Geographic specials to have a healthy fear of great white sharks. But I am not sitting at my computer right now shivering in fear of them! Why not? Because there aren't any around, of course.

On the other hand, put me in the ocean (especially at night!) and have somebody yell, "Shark!" and you'd be watching every Olympic swimming record smashed as I headed for shore. Why? Because suddenly I would be vulnerable—the present threat of a shark attack would exist.

Once I got up on the beach (and I mean *way up* on the beach!), would I be afraid anymore? Of course not! Once I got out of the water and up on the sand, I would be away from the presence of any sharks . . . even *sand* sharks!

Now suppose I went to a natural science museum and in one of the rooms was a twenty-five-foot great white mounted on the wall. Imagine I walked up to it and even stuck my hand in its mouth. Would I be afraid to do that? Naturally, no. Why not? Obviously, because it's dead. Even though it is *present,* it is not *powerful.*

So how do I overcome my fear of great white sharks? By

staying out of water where they might be lurking (removing their presence) and by limiting my close encounters to those that are stuffed or on the other side of glass aquariums (removing their power to harm me).

And those principles remain true of every fear object you might have. If you can eliminate just one of those two factors—presence or power—you will eliminate the hold that object of fear has over you!

The Big Three

There is a trio of fear objects that tend to frighten most people. Yet the Bible tells us not to fear them. If we can conquer our fear of these three areas, we can go a long way toward living a free and productive life. Then we will experience more of the powerful freedom God has for us—freedom to walk with Him and know and do His will.

Let's look at each of these three main fear objects one by one and see what God says about them.

The first fear is *fear of man*. Scripture says that "Fear of man will prove to be a snare, but whoever trusts in the LORD is kept safe" (Prov. 29:25). The fear of what people will do to us can easily keep us from doing what God wants for us. In high school, my (Rich) body went crazy. In about a year, I shot up from 5'8" and 120 pounds to 6'2" . . . 120 pounds! I wasn't skinny; I was *skeletal*.

Everywhere I went I heard people snickering at me (even when they were laughing at something else!). I was called every name in the book. It hurt a lot. I became so afraid that no one would want me to sit with them at lunchtime that I avoided the school cafeteria all together. I would bring a sack lunch to school, find a vacant classroom, and eat lunch there—by myself.

I didn't know Christ as a high school student. I became a Christian in college, and since then He has set me free from my fear of people as I have opened my heart to Him and His truth.

How has He done that? By assuring me of His love and protection. Jesus said in John 15:9, "As the Father has loved me, so have I loved you. Now remain in my love." The more I have come to know how completely and deeply I am loved by the God who made me, the more convinced I have become of my value as a person.

The assurance of God's love for me acts as a shield when people criticize, reject, or embarrass me. As long as I know that God accepts me just as I am (and He does, in Christ!), I can keep on keeping on with life, even in the midst of pain. Psalm 118:5-8 says:

> *In my anguish I cried to the LORD,*
> *and he answered by setting me free.*
> *The LORD is with me; I will not be afraid.*
> *What can man do to me?*
> *The LORD is with me; he is my helper.*
> *I will look in triumph on my enemies.*
> *It is better to take refuge in the LORD*
> *than to trust in man.*

You might be saying, "There's a lot that people can do to me! My coach can cut me from the team. My boss can fire me. My friends can reject me. Other people can spread rumors about me and ruin my reputation. Some mugger on the street could put a knife in my back!"

All those things *are* possibilities. How, then, can we overcome the fear of man that constantly seeks to overcome us? We could choose to become hermits and withdraw from the *presence* of people, but then how could we act as the salt of the earth and light of the world? No, God wants us to stick around and love people and show them Jesus.

The secret to conquering the fear of man is in removing

the *power* that people have over you. It comes from making Christ your Lord, seeing Him as your life, and realizing that no matter what happens, He will take care of you. The apostle Peter came to realize firsthand that ultimately nothing matters apart from Christ and what He chooses to give us. He wrote:

> *Dear friends, do not be surprised at the painful trial you are suffering, as though something strange were happening to you. But rejoice that you participate in the sufferings of Christ, so that you may be overjoyed when his glory is revealed. If you are insulted because of the name of Christ, you are blessed, for the Spirit of glory and of God rests on you. If you suffer, it should not be as a murderer or thief or any other kind of criminal, or even as a meddler. However, if you suffer as a Christian, do not be ashamed, but praise God that you bear that name. (1 Peter 4:12-16)*

The Bible in fact promises that "everyone who wants to live a godly life in Christ Jesus will be persecuted" (2 Tim. 3:12). You can count on it. But that should not shock or confuse you. Jesus lived the perfect life and people still rejected Him. It should come as no surprise then if the same thing happens to you! God, however, promises to fill you with a deep inner joy and peace that will enable you to endure (Matt. 5:10-12).

Are you afraid to witness for Christ for fear of being laughed at or rejected? Be a God-pleaser, not a man-pleaser. Does God want you to bring the good news to a dying world? Of course. Will He be with you as you share your faith? You bet. Is He able to comfort you should you be rejected? You better believe it.

Yes, you can keep quiet and stay safe, locked in the coffin of your own fear. Or you can step out in faith and break those chains and watch the almighty God of the universe use you for His glory! The choice is yours.

Peter caved in to the fear of people, didn't he? And he knew the awful feeling of having let fear rob him of faith when he denied Jesus three times. Later he learned that it was worth losing everything to walk with Christ, and he wrote:

> *Who is going to harm you if you are eager to do good? But even if you should suffer for what is right, you are blessed. "Do not fear what they fear; do not be frightened." But in your hearts set apart Christ as Lord. Always be prepared to give an answer to everyone who asks you to give the reason for the hope that you have. But do this with gentleness and respect. (1 Peter 3:13-15)*

The second object in the trio of fear is the *fear of death*. Many of the horrible, paralyzing phobias that people have can be traced to a root fear of death.

Is it possible to escape death? No, for Scripture clearly teaches that "it is appointed for men to die once and after this comes judgment" (Heb. 9:27 NASB).

It is not possible to remove the *presence* of death from our lives. In fact, we have no guarantees that we will be alive one minute from now. God alone holds our lives in His hands, and He ain't lettin' on how much time we've got!

Somehow, then, if we are to conquer our fear of death, we have to remove its *power* from us. And of course, that was done when Christ took upon Himself the sentence of death and died for our sins on the cross. Three days later He exploded free from death's chains and came back to life ... forever.

The apostle Paul was aware of the incredible truth that Christ rose victorious from the grave. And that's not all, folks. Because He conquered death, so will all who belong to Him!

Barely containing his joy, Paul wrote:

"Death has been swallowed up in victory."
"Where, O death, is your victory?
Where, O death, is your sting?"
The sting of death is sin, and the power of sin is the law. But thanks be to God! He gives us the victory through our Lord Jesus Christ.(1 Cor. 15:54-57)

Everyone who has Christ has eternal life (1 John 5:11-13), and even death itself can't separate us from God's love (Rom. 8:38). In fact, for the Christian, physical death becomes the gateway into the presence of Christ Himself!

Paul said, "For to me, to live is Christ and to die is gain" (Phil. 1:21). Why could Paul make such a statement? Isn't dying the worst thing that can happen to you? No, for the believer in Christ, dying is the *best thing* that can happen to you. For heaven is our home, and dying is the homecoming that will bring us safely into the arms of the One who has gone to prepare a place for us, Jesus Christ.

What about for you? Complete this statement:

For me, to live is _____ and to die is _____ .

You see, if you are living for *money,* then dying would be loss. If you are living for your *girlfriend* or *boyfriend,* then dying would be loss. If you are living for *success, popularity, athletic achievements,* or *anything else apart from Christ,* then for you, dying would be loss. And the prospect of dying will bring fear.

If you are a Christian, your life is hidden with Christ in God (Col. 3:3). In fact, Christ *is* your life. Therefore, set your heart on things above, where Christ is, not on earthly things. When you finally settle this issue, you will be free from the fear of death. And the one who is free from the fear of death is finally free to truly live life today.

The *fear of Satan* is the last of the trio. Many people watch movies such as *The Exorcist* or *The Omen* or countless other B-grade videos that rent for two bucks at the local store, and they become afraid of the devil.

There is no verse in the Bible that instructs the believer in Christ to be afraid of Satan. But we are to be on the alert, as 1 Peter 5:7-9 warns: "Cast all your anxiety on him [God] because he cares for you. Be self-controlled and alert. Your enemy the devil prowls around like a roaring lion looking for someone to devour. Resist him, standing firm in the faith."

A lion has such a terrible roar that it can paralyze its prey. That is the devil's tactic as well. He tries to frighten us so that we will be frozen in fear rather than fearless in faith. Then he can bully us around.

I (Rich) was on a summer missions project one year at a beach resort. There was a considerable amount of rebellion, lying, and bitterness among some of the guys. It was a bad situation, and I'm sure the devil was behind much of it.

I didn't know a whole lot about my authority in Christ, and so I wasn't prepared for Satan's attack when it came. I woke up in the middle of the night and perched in mid-air above my head was an evil, mocking face. And it wasn't one of the teenage boys either!

Being the strong, red-blooded American Christian man that I was, I took immediate action. I freaked out, pulled the sheet over my head, and started praying like crazy! Prayer was a good start, but I could have done more.

In *The Bondage Breaker* I (Neil) give the following illustration. When I was a young boy on the farm, our neighbors had a yappy little dog that scared the socks off me. I recall one day when my brother, father, and I drove over to their farm. As soon as we got out of the pickup, that dog came roaring around the corner barking like crazy.

Guess who the dog chased? Terrorized, I ran! I found sanctuary on top of the pickup. My brother and father stood right next to the dog, who was barking only at me. It didn't chase or bother them one bit. What power did that dog have to put me on top of that pickup?

It had no power at all. It was a puny little runt! The only power it had was the power I gave it. I'll tell you how I ended up on top of the truck. That dog manipulated my mind, my will, my emotions, and my muscles. My dad thought it was a little embarrassing. He wanted me to stand my ground.

The next time we went to that farm, I worked up my courage and when the dog came after me I kicked a rock at it. To my great relief, it put its tail between its legs and took off.

What a great picture of our battle against Satan. He gives the appearance of being very ferocious, but he's already been defeated and disarmed by Jesus on the cross (Col. 2:13-15)! As we live our lives under the authority of the One who has all authority (the Lord Jesus), we can tell the enemy to leave and he must go. James summed it up best when he wrote: "'God opposes the proud but gives grace to the humble.' Submit yourselves, then, to God. Resist the devil, and he will flee from you" (James 4:6-7).

Did you catch the order in that Scripture passage? It is crucial. *First* you must submit to God's rule in your life in a spirit of humility. *Then* you will be able to resist the devil, and he will indeed flee from you. If, however, you are living in pride and not following Jesus as Lord, you can resist the devil until you're blue in the face and he won't go. I (Rich) should have confronted the demonic spirit in my bedroom and ordered it to leave in Jesus' name.

The A-Word

Maybe you noticed that right before Peter described the devil as a roaring lion (1 Peter 5:8), he talked about anxiety (1 Peter 5:7). One of Satan's favorite tools is the common psychological disorder called "anxiety attacks." In most cases there is no specific object of fear, just an overwhelming sense of terror. In those situations it is almost always a demonic attack.

Because of the nature of my ministry I (Neil) have had several such attacks. I'm not by nature a timid person, but I have awakened at night in terror. Since I know what is going on, I know how to get rid of it.

Most people try to respond physically but can't. Anxiety attacks often feel like intense pressure on the chest or like something grabbing your throat. Because you may not be able to move or even cry out, you can feel overwhelmed. Fighting in the power of the flesh will not cut it here, as 2 Corinthians 10:4 reveals: "The weapons of our warfare are not of the flesh, but divinely powerful for the destruction of fortresses" (NASB).

What do we do, then, when we encounter a direct attack from Satan? The devil is not able to touch our core identity in Christ (1 John 5:18). That is who we are. We are *in Christ*, and Christ has all authority. The Lord Jesus Christ is the Commander in Chief and we are His generals. Because of Jesus' victory over Satan on the cross, demonic powers have been defeated, and they must bow before their Conquering Victor and His troops!

As we silently submit our lives to Christ and acknowledge His lordship, we will be free to speak. All we have to say is, "Jesus!" and the attack will usually cease. But we do need to *say* it. The devil cannot perfectly read our minds, so he is under no obligation to obey our thoughts.

This point of *verbally* resisting the devil cannot be overstated. If there was one person who would have been able to resist Satan with His thoughts, it would have been Jesus Himself. But each time in the wilderness, when the devil tempted Him, the Lord *spoke out loud* to Satan, quoting the word of God as found in the book of Deuteronomy.

The result of this battle in the wilderness was that the devil departed, knowing that he was licked. He fled from Jesus, and he will flee from you as you follow the strategy of James 4:7.

Satan loves to do everything in the darkness. God wants us to walk in the light as He Himself is in the light (1 John 1:7). When a temptation, accusing thought, or fearful attack of Satan comes into your mind, don't be intimidated. The devil wants you to keep it inside your head and become worried and fearful about it. Don't do that. Get it out in the light! If you are alone and under attack, say out loud, "That's a lie, Satan, and I renounce it! I choose to believe the truth."

Then quote a Scripture that pertains to the attack. You would be wise to commit to memory some Bible verses that relate to areas of weakness in your life.

The devil cannot stand before the truth of God's Word spoken out loud by a child of God (no matter how young!) who is living in submission to Jesus Christ!

There is only One that the Bible says we are to fear, and that is God Himself. As I said before, the fear of the Lord is the beginning of knowledge (Prov. 1:7) and wisdom (Prov. 9:10). It is our motivation to stay away from evil (Prov. 16:6) and provides a strong fortress of security in life (Prov. 14:26).

What does it mean to fear God? It means that we hold Him in the highest honor and respect. We recognize that He is the Lord, the Holy One, awesome in power, majesty, and glory. And we are aware that the living God is with us, here and now and always. It doesn't mean that we are afraid of

Him, as 1 John 4:18 makes clear: "There is no fear in love. But perfect love drives out fear, because fear has to do with punishment. The one who fears is not made perfect in love."

God does not want us to have some kind of cringing fear of Him, like a dog that fears being beaten by its cruel owner. That kind of fear involves punishment, John says. But Jesus already took upon Himself the punishment and judgment that we deserve. He said on the cross, "It is finished!" Therefore, we can approach God boldly—not in cowering fear but in awe of His incredible greatness. That is what the Bible means when it speaks of "the fear of the Lord." And that kind of fear is the healthiest fear of all.

Since God is *always present* and *all-powerful,* He indeed is to be feared, as the book of Isaiah says so clearly:

> *The LORD spoke to me with his strong hand upon me, warning me not to follow the way of this people. He said: . . .*
> *"Do not fear what they fear,*
> *and do not dread it.*
> *The LORD Almighty is the one you are to regard as holy,*
> *he is the one you are to fear,*
> *he is the one you are to dread,*
> *and he will be a sanctuary." (Isa. 8:11-14)*

When you fear God in this healthy, biblical way, you are not driven away from Him, but drawn toward Him! And in that drawing, you find that He is a sanctuary from all other fears. Indeed the fear of the Lord is the fear that expels all other (unhealthy) fears in life!

Worship God in reverent awe for His glory and majesty. Obey the Lord, for He is holy. Rid yourself of every other god, for the Lord is a jealous God. Serve Him in love so that one day you can hear Him say, "Well done, good and faithful servant. Enter into the joy of your Lord."

Do you want to know the will of God for your life?

Cultivate the fear of the Lord in your life. It is the *beginning* of wisdom.

Help Is on the Way _____

At the end of this chapter you will find a "Phobia Finder." It will help you put a finger on any fears in your life and help you resolve them. Let's go through it briefly so you understand the process.

First, *analyze your fear*. Identify all fear objects. Ask the Lord to show you what you are afraid of. He will. Remember, fear is not from God, but He has given us a spirit of power, love, and a sound mind (2 Tim. 1:7).

Ask the Lord to reveal *when* the fear began. Sin that is unconfessed can give the devil a foothold. For example, acts of sexual immorality or having an abortion, things the Bible says are wrong, could be the root cause of anxiety attacks. Perhaps there was a tragedy (such as a death or divorce) in your family that began a pattern of fear in your life. If the Lord reveals any sin on your part that helped bring fear into your life, confess it to God. Don't make excuses. Proverbs 28:13 says, "He who conceals his sins does not prosper, but whoever confesses and renounces them finds mercy."

Then, *determine any way in which fear has been your Lord instead of Christ*. Again, ask the Lord to reveal the truth here. In what ways have you allowed fear to keep you from doing what's right? In what ways have you allowed fear to bully you into doing what's wrong? Have you compromised your witness for Christ?

If we fear men, we will constantly be taking the path of least resistance, afraid of losing respect, friendships, opportunities for advancement, and so on. Those who choose this way of life will one day find they have lost all respect anyway—from others and themselves.

Confess your sin of allowing fear rather than the Spirit

of God to control you. Specifically confess any sins of commission, omission, or compromise that the Lord reveals to your mind. Choose the fear of the Lord. Set apart Christ as the Lord of your life. Make God your sanctuary and commit yourself to living a responsible life according to His will.

Third, *work out a plan of responsible action.* Ask the Lord to show you what His will is for you. How does He want you to walk by faith instead of fear? If it is safe to do so, you may need to confront your fear object face-to-face.

That's what I (Rich) had to do. I used to be afraid of heights, but I wanted to go skiing. The first time I rode a chairlift, I was scared to death. I caught my ski in the ramp when I got on the lift and came close to falling off the blasted thing!

For five years I avoided skiing out of fear. Then the Lord spoke to me through 1 Corinthians 6:12, "'Everything is permissible for me'—but I will not be mastered by any-thing." I was mastered by my fear of chairlifts, and I knew it.

I had to face that fear one cold day in the Colorado Rocky Mountains, and I did it! I was so excited that I don't think I touched the snow as I skied down that mountain.

Steps four and five are: *Prepare yourself for your time of confronting your fear object* and then *carry out the plan.* As I prepared to hop on that chairlift the second time, I made sure I knew how to do it! I got in position well in advance of its "rear assault" so I would not be caught off guard. Avoiding as many surprises as possible is very helpful at this stage.

To make sure I followed through with my plan, I had someone with me. She had no idea I was scared to death and in fact, she was looking to me for courage! What a bluffer I was!

Once I got on, I was ready with plenty of songs of praise

to sing to keep my attention focused on God. And it worked!

Do the thing you fear the most, and the death of that fear is certain. Fear is really like a mirage. The closer you get to it, the more it evaporates into nothingness. Satan wants you to picture your fears as bigger than life, and they will seem that way if you try to avoid them.

The psalmist captured the heart of walking by faith, not fear when he wrote:

> God is our refuge and strength,
> an ever-present help in trouble.
> Therefore we will not fear, though the earth give way
> and the mountains fall into the heart of the sea,
> though its waters roar and foam
> and the mountains quake with their surging. (Ps. 46:1-3)

All of us know what it's like to be afraid, but how much is fear controlling our lives? We need to stop and pray to the One who says, "Do not fear, for I am with you; do not be dismayed, for I am your God." He promises to strengthen us, help us and uphold us with His righteous right hand (Isa. 41:10).

Without a complete dependence on the Lord, we can become easily frozen in the paralyzing grip of fear. Fearing anything but the Lord will keep us from knowing His will. With His help we can, even now, begin to feel the warm breeze of His presence blow over us, melting away the chilling fears in our lives. Will you join us as we pray?

> Dear heavenly Father, You are my shield and my fortress and the strength of my life. I choose to walk by faith in You instead of giving in to my fears. I thank You that You have not given me a spirit of fear, but of power, love, and a sound mind.
> I decide today to renounce the fear of men, the fear of

death, the fear of Satan, and any other fear object in my life. I choose instead to make Jesus Christ the Lord of my life. Teach me the fear of the Lord, so that I may worship You and obey You. You are my sanctuary and I need no other.

By Your presence and power, Lord, I commit myself to being always ready to tell people of my faith in You. I look forward to the boldness You will give me through the filling of the Holy Spirit. Amen.

Phobia Finder _____

1. Analyze your fear.
   a. Identify all fear objects. (Ask the Lord to reveal to you everything you are afraid of.)
   b. When did each fear first show up? (Ask the Lord to show you.)
   c. What events triggered the beginning of that fear? (Ask God to bring any memories back to your mind.)

2. Determine any way in which fear has been your Lord instead of Christ.
   a. In what ways does your fear
      - prevent you from doing what's right?
      - compel you to do what's wrong?
      - cause you to compromise your witness for Christ?
   b. Confess any way in which you have allowed fear to control you.
   c. Make Christ your Lord and commit yourself to being obedient to whatever He shows you to do.

3. Work out a plan of responsible action, including a plan to confront your fear object face-to-face, if it is safe to do so.

4. Prepare yourself for the time of confronting your fear object by fixing your eyes on God's love and protection of you.

5. Carry out the plan. Having a trusted friend with you may help.

~~~ PART 2 ~~~

Principles for Discerning God's Will

~~~

The Bottom Line for You and Me

"How can I be sure of what God is saying to me?" "How can I know for certain what He wants me to do?" These are two of the most common questions that Christian teenagers ask today. Why? Because they lie at the root of all decision making that the sincere follower of Christ has to do in his or her life.

This problem is not new. It has been around for thousands of years. In Jesus' day, the debate was raging: Is this Jesus fellow from God or not? Can we trust His teaching? Some people concluded, "He is a good man," while others disagreed, saying, "No, he deceives the people" (John 7:12).

When the Jews heard His teaching and asked, "How did this man get such learning without studying?" Jesus responded:

My teaching is not my own. It comes from him who sent me. If anyone chooses to do God's will, he will find out whether my teaching comes from God or whether I speak on my own. (John 7:16-17)

In essence, Jesus is saying, "Do you want to know the will of God? Make the decision up front to *do* God's will, and God will show you what it is!"

But how do we come to the point of being willing to accept God's plan for our lives—lock, stock, and barrel? Good question. However, before we get to the specifics of God's plan for *you*, we need to get a handle on God's plan for *the world*. After all, you are a part of God's world and so am I.

God's Plan for the World _____

What would you say is God's will for the world? What is His greatest desire for the human race? Without even realizing it, you've probably prayed for this exact thing many times in the Lord's Prayer: *Our Father, which art in heaven, hallowed be Thy name. Thy kingdom come, Thy will be done on earth as it is in heaven.*

Did you catch it? Jesus instructed us in that prayer (Matt. 6:9-13) to pray that God's will would be done on earth just like it is done in heaven. And what is His will? *Thy kingdom come.*

I don't think Jesus is simply telling us to pray for His return. He is telling us to pray for His rule (kingdom) to come to individuals, families, churches, communities, and even entire nations! That is the primary focus of God's work here on the blue planet. Check out the following Scriptures:

- The Lord is not slow in keeping his promise, as some

understand slowness. He is patient with you, not wanting anyone to perish, but everyone to come to repentance. (2 Peter 3:9)

- This is good [praying for people], and pleases God our Savior, who wants all men to be saved and to come to a knowledge of the truth. (1 Tim. 2:3-4)
- For the Son of Man [Jesus] came to seek and to save what was lost. (Luke 19:10)
- He who does what is sinful is of the devil, because the devil has been sinning from the beginning. The reason the Son of God appeared was to destroy the devil's work. (1 John 3:8)
- And I [Jesus] tell you that you are Peter, and on this rock I will build my church, and the gates of Hades will not overcome it. (Matt. 16:18)

Let's sum up what we've just read: God's will for the world is that people would come to know Jesus Christ in order to be made spiritually alive and be saved from sin, so that they could be set free from the devil's control and become a part of God's great building project: the church.

So whatever God may have in store for you, He is going to want you to be part of this great plan. If you are not willing to "get with the program" that He has for the world, how can you expect Him to show you your specific role in that plan?

Okay, let's bring it down a little closer to home. We have begun to see what God's plan is for the world—the coming of His kingdom to human hearts. What does that mean to the individual believer? What is God's will for each Christian?

God's Will for You _____

Simply stated: God's will for each Christian is that he or

she become more and more like Jesus and do good works of love so that people will be pointed to God. Consider the next set of Scripture verses:

- For those God foreknew he also predestined to be conformed to the likeness of his Son, that he might be the firstborn among many brothers. (Rom. 8:29)
- The goal of our instruction is love from a pure heart and a good conscience and a sincere faith. (1 Tim. 1:5 NASB)
- You are the salt of the earth. But if the salt loses its saltiness, how can it be made salty again? It is no longer good for anything, except to be thrown out and trampled by men. You are the light of the world. A city on a hill cannot be hidden. Neither do people light a lamp and put it under a bowl. Instead they put it on its stand, and it gives light to everyone in the house. In the same way, let your light shine before men, that they may see your good deeds and praise your Father in heaven. (Matt. 5:13-16)

God is in the character-building business, and when it comes to our lives, that is His main concern. The Bible, for instance, says nothing about which college you should attend, but it says an awful lot about what kind of student you should be!

You see, God is most concerned about what you are becoming on the inside (your character). Why is that? Simply because God knows that if you are becoming the right kind of person on the inside, that will automatically show up in how you live on the outside.

As a college junior, I (Rich) thought I had the world by the tail. I was studying at Penn State to be a weather forecaster and getting good grades. By that time I had gained a lot of weight, so I felt good about my appearance. I worked as a lifeguard and a swimming instructor, so money was no problem. My college profs liked me and so did most of the guys in my dorm. From all outward appearances, I was headed for success in all areas. But I was not happy.

During my freshman year I had opened my heart to Christ, but unless I happened to tell someone I was a Christian (which was rare), no one would have guessed. I was constantly making fun of people in a cruel way. Sure I was a funny guy, but the "fun" was always at someone else's expense.

One day I went to get my yearbook picture taken. Being kind of a rebel, I was dressed in a jacket and tie, shorts, and tennis shoes! The photographer was a loud, backslapping kind of guy, and I liked him. When it was time to snap the pictures, he told me to say, not "Cheese!" but an obscenity.

I went along with him, not wanting to make a scene. I guess I smiled when I said the words, because he seemed happy with the shots.

"Y'know, Rich," he said cheerfully as I was leaving, "you're a man after my own heart. The last person in here didn't want to say what you said [the obscenity]. He wanted to say 'Jesus' instead."

I felt as if a knife had gone straight into my heart. I grunted something in response and bolted out of there as fast as I could.

God broke me there and showed me that what was missing from my life was a sold-out commitment to Him. I made the decision then and there to go all the way with Jesus and to never deny my Lord or compromise my walk with Him like that again.

The lordship of Christ is a "watershed" issue that every believer in Jesus must face head on. There are no detours around it or convenient tunnels through it. Who will *really* be the Lord of your life? Your decision in this matter will determine the whole course of your life.

The Little Things _____

There is another principle concerning the will of God that will be helpful for you to understand. This important truth comes from Luke 16:10: "Whoever can be trusted with very little can also be trusted with much, and whoever is dishonest with very little will also be dishonest with much."

The context of the verse has to do with the use of money, and that is a very important truth in and of itself. But the application is much broader and could be stated like this: If you obey God in little things now, He will trust you with much bigger things later. But if you prove unreliable in the little things now, that indicates that you will not be dependable with bigger things in the future.

Here is a short checklist you can use to see if you are being faithful to do what God wants in the "little things" He brings your way:

- When your parents tell you to do something, do you respond right away or do you put them off for as long as possible?
- Do you join in when other students make fun of teachers and other students or do you refuse to be a part of those kinds of conversations?
- Can your word be trusted? Do you say what you mean and mean what you say? Or do you make a habit of lying, exaggerating, or breaking promises?
- Do you seek to do an excellent job in your work at school or on the job or do you do just enough to get by?
- Are you seeking to be a loving witness for Christ in your home, school, etc. or are you just biding your time until you can get out on your own?
- If you drive, do you obey the traffic laws, including speed limits, or do you just drive as you please?

Society today expects teenagers to be disrespectful, lazy, sloppy goof-offs. As a Christian young person, you have the incredible opportunity and responsibility to prove them wrong! But your actions will speak much louder than your words, as Proverbs 20:11 wisely says: "It is by his deeds that a lad distinguishes himself / If his conduct is pure and right" (NASB).

If you show yourself faithful in the things that matter, people will begin to notice. And you better believe God will too! Your boss may give you a promotion or a raise. Your teacher may recommend you for a special honor or award. Your parents will feel the freedom to give you increasing responsibilities . . . and privileges. And perhaps most important of all, you will be developing the kind of character that God honors and uses for His glory!

King David is a classic example. As a boy, he had the lonely job of shepherding sheep. And sheep aren't exactly the most exciting companions in the world. But because of his faithfulness in that "little thing," God was able to develop crucial character qualities in David's life.

He learned firsthand of God's shepherd-heart for His people and wrote about it in Psalm 23. Eventually, the Lord called David to be the shepherd (king) of Israel. Why David? Because he had allowed God to mold him and teach him important lessons about being king during those early years "down on the farm" with the sheep. His faithfulness in the "small" task of herding sheep led to his reward: kingship, the largest of tasks!

Where to Begin _____

The apostle Paul instructed his spiritual son, Timothy (who was a young man), on how to live successfully in this world: "Let no one look down on your youthfulness, but rather in speech, conduct, love, faith and purity, show yourself an example of those who believe" (1 Tim. 4:12 NASB).

Cultivate faithfulness to God and His will in these five areas during your teenage years, and you will reap a harvest of fruitfulness for Him in the days to come.

Speech. Don't let your mouth be a tool for Satan's wrecking crew. Let your words build up others and encourage them. Avoid gossip and profanity. Only God can bridle your tongue; ask Him to begin doing that today.

Conduct. Learn to be submissive to the human authorities over you, especially your parents. God has placed them there for your protection. Be a person that others can and do trust. Remember that before honor comes humility and with humility comes wisdom.

Love. This is the mark of a true disciple of Christ. Spend intimate time with God regularly and grow in your love for Him. Ask Him to fill your heart with love for other people, especially those who irritate you or treat you unfairly.

Faith. As you grow to know and love God more, you will be able to trust Him more. Ask Him to show you how to have an impact for Christ in your home, church, and school. Then step out by faith in His power and wisdom and watch Him work!

Purity. Make the rock-solid choice to stay sexually pure until marriage. Ask others to pray for you. Don't do anything or go anywhere that puts you in a position to compromise. If you have failed in this area already, confess your sin, break off any sinful relationship, and learn to walk with the Father, who loves, forgives, and accepts you just as you are in Christ.

How Others Paved the Way _____

It's not easy to choose the highway of holiness, that's

true. But many young people before you have walked that road and reaped great blessings from God.

That's why God wrote down the stories of young people in the Bible who beat the odds and walked with God no matter what the world, the flesh, and the devil threw their way.

Check out the life of Joseph (Gen. 37-50). It may be the most awesome short story ever written—and it's all true.

Get to know Daniel and his three young friends (the book of Daniel) and watch how God used their faith to rock and roll the most powerful empire of that day.

Read about young Queen Esther (the book of Esther) and her gutsy life of faith in the face of death. The ending to that true story will leave you shaking your head in wonder at the power of God to protect His people.

Another young person, Dwight Moody, was an overweight, uneducated shoe salesman who wanted to teach a youth Sunday school class. He had gathered a group of street kids who were willing to attend. But the church leader he approached told him to go find his own class and to keep the kids away from the church until they learned to behave.

And that's exactly what he did! He taught them on his own, and soon he had won to Christ several hundred youths and was helping them grow in their faith.

Although he had never gone to seminary, Dwight felt God's call to preach the gospel. Early one morning he and some of his buddies got together in a hay field to pray, confess their sins, and give themselves to the Lord for whatever He desired. One of the men, Henry Varley, said, "The world has yet to see what God can do with and for and through and in a man who is fully and wholly consecrated to Him."[1]

The rest is history. D. L. Moody was certainly one of the greatest evangelists this country has ever seen. Thousands upon thousands came to Christ through his ministry both in the United States and in Great Britain. He even spoke to packed houses in the most prestigious universities in England, including Cambridge and Oxford! And it all started when Mr. Moody decided to "bloom where he was planted"—pulling together a Sunday school class for out-of-control street kids in Chicago!

Jesus' disciples Peter and John were arrested for "disturbing the peace." They had been used by God to heal a crippled beggar (Acts 3) and had taken the opportunity to teach and preach the gospel of Jesus. Outraged, the religious leaders fired question-bullets at the two disciples. Peter gently but firmly silenced them with his Spirit-filled words of power. The words of Acts 4:13 send chills up my spine: "When they [the Jewish leaders] saw the courage of Peter and John and realized that they were unschooled, ordinary men, they were astonished and they took note that these men had been with Jesus."

I wonder. If you or I were called on the carpet and backed into a corner, what would those who attack us see? Would they see timid, noncommitted young people? Would they see ordinary men (and women)? Or would they see extraordinary men and women alive in Jesus Christ and unwilling to compromise what they believe, no matter what the cost?

It all starts with becoming sold out to God and His will. There are two words in the English language that should never go together. They are No and Lord. You see, if Jesus is truly the Lord, and we are totally His, that means He calls the shots. Our response to Him as the One in charge should always be, "Yes, Lord!"

Most of us, however, would like to know ahead of time what His will is, and then we would gladly let the Lord know our decision! But the Lord just doesn't work that way.

God has set before you and before me an open door. But it is impossible to see what is on the other side of the door until we walk through the doorway—all the way.

How can we come to the point of saying, "All right, Lord. My life is Yours. I am willing to follow wherever You lead, whenever You lead, and however You lead"? The key is found in Romans 12:1-2 (NASB):

I urge you therefore, brethren, by the mercies of God, to present your bodies a living and holy sacrifice, acceptable to God, which is your spiritual service of worship. And do not be conformed to this world, but be transformed by the renewing of your mind, that you may prove what the will of God is, that which is good and acceptable and perfect.

Did you get it? It's right there. God's will is what? That which is *good and acceptable and perfect!* That's the key that enables you to walk through the open door.

The devil wants you to believe that God cannot be trusted. Don't believe his lies. *God's will is good.*

The devil wants you to believe that you won't like what God has for you. Don't believe his lies. *God's will is acceptable.* The devil wants you to believe that you can't handle God's will. It will be too tough, he says. Don't believe his lies. *God's will is perfect.*

In the last half of the nineteenth century, George Mueller founded the Bristol Orphan Home. It became known around the world as one of the most incredible works of God's grace and man's faith in history.

For years, without a single plea for money, George Mueller saw that hundreds of children were fed, clothed, and educated. The orphanage was run completely on faith and prayer.

Mueller captured the bottom line for you and me when he wrote:

I seek in the beginning to get my heart in such a state that it has no will of its own in regard to a given matter. Nine-tenths of the trouble with people is just here. Nine-tenths of the difficulties are overcome when our hearts are ready to do the Lord's will. When one is truly in this state, it is usually but a little way to the knowledge of what His will is.[2]

Joshua gave this challenge thousands of years ago, but it still stands today: "Choose for yourselves this day whom you will serve" (Josh. 24:15). Will you serve God or someone or something else? That's the bottom line.

Knowing that "what's on the other side of the door" comes from the heart and hand of our loving, all-wise, all-powerful heavenly Father, will you pray this prayer with us?

Dear heavenly Father, once and for all this day I choose to make You and You alone the Lord of my life. Your love for me is even greater than my love for myself. Your knowledge and understanding of my life are far greater than my own. And Your power is all-power, dwarfing my puny strength.

Forgive me for the times I have acted as my own god and tried to write the script for my life by myself. Forgive me for ever doubting that Your will is anything but good, acceptable, and perfect for me. I don't want to be squeezed into the world's mold anymore. I want to become like Jesus.

Teach me to be faithful to what You have called me to do. Make me a person who in speech, conduct, love, faith, and purity is truly an example of what a Christian should be.

Please fill me with the Holy Spirit. I can't do any of this on my own power. May Your kingdom come in me. May Your will be done in me here on earth as it is in heaven. I submit to You, my King. In Jesus' name, amen.

CHAPTER 7

The Bottom Line for God

It was May 11. My (Rich) birthday. All my buddies on the dorm floor where I lived at Penn State were in a partying mood, and so was I. Even though I had received Christ about four and a half months earlier, knowing and doing God's will were the farthest things from my mind that night. After all, it was the weekend, I was nineteen years old, and there was plenty of beer to go around . . . all paid for by somebody else! Who could be expected to do anything except party hearty?

Early in the evening the warning shout rang out. "Rich, your brother's coming!"

Oh great, I thought. To me, my brother was the Second Coming of the apostle Paul—*not* the person I wanted to see right then.

I quickly hid my bottle of beer and tried to look sober. As drunk as I already was, that was about as futile as a woman about to have a baby trying not to look pregnant!

I could see the hurt in my brother's eyes as he handed me my birthday present. I opened it in front of all my friends and wished I could have crawled under a rock. It was a Christian book.

I slurred a "thank you" to him, and he quickly (and mercifully) left. Talk about a room full of uncomfortable people breathing a sigh of relief. And I was sighing the loudest.

It didn't take long for the party to get back into full swing, and that included my drinking.

Somewhere in the middle of the night one of my friends came up with the brainy idea of wrapping me up in a bedsheet and putting me on the dorm elevator. Too drunk to fight back, I had no choice but to let them dump me there. Then they pushed the button for every floor in my dorm, and left to go back to the party.

I was the life of the party on every floor. The elevator would stop, open its doors revealing its mummified passenger, close its doors, and move on to its next stop. Everyone had a good laugh over it, except me. I felt completely humiliated.

Finally the elevator made it back down to my floor, and I was able to crawl out. By that time I was feeling pretty sick to my stomach, so I dragged myself over to a corner of the lobby and just lay there trying hard not to throw up.

Somewhere around two or three in the morning, still on the verge of vomiting, I started crawling back to my room. I remember praying, "Lord, if You keep me from throwing up all over the hall I'll turn my life back over to You."

To my amazement, I was able to make it back to my room

and crawl up onto my mattress. My feet and half of my legs were dangling over the end of the bed, but I didn't care.

Suddenly my friends burst into the room, laughing. They grabbed me by the feet and shoved me full force onto the bed, accidentally smashing my head into the wall. I should have had a concussion, I hit so hard. But I couldn't feel a thing.

Relieved that they hadn't hurt me, my buddies left me alone with my now wide-awake, Christian roommate. I was ready for hellfire and brimstone from him, and I would have deserved it. But it never came.

After a while he quietly asked me, "Rich, do you think this is glorifying God?"

"No," I mumbled. What *could* I say? It was obvious I was a spiritual wreck.

But I had made a promise to God, and I intended to keep my end of the bargain. Soon after, with His help, I was able to leave the drinking, partying scene behind forever.

How about your life? Is it your goal to bring glory to God? Are you finding it at all hard (like I did) to live a life pleasing to Him?

One thing is for certain, the will of God will always bring glory to God, because glorifying God is the bottom line for Him.

What does it mean to glorify something? It means to direct attention to something in such a way that people give honor, praise, or worship to it. For example, picture in your mind a large, beautifully cut diamond sitting on a blue velvet cloth in a dark corner of a museum. The gem is priceless in value, but no one even notices until a spotlight is turned directly on it. Suddenly, heads turn and all eyes are drawn to that precious jewel.

What did the light do? Did it increase the value of the diamond? No, it didn't. But it pointed people to it and revealed its beauty so that they were able to marvel at its glory. The light glorified the diamond.

Had you been in that room, would you have been staring up at the lightbulb saying, "What a wonderful spotlight"? Of course not. You would have been gazing in wonder at that incredible diamond sparkling in its radiance.

We can do the same thing for God—point to His radiance. And, incredibly, the different Persons of the Trinity (God the Father, God the Son, and God the Holy Spirit) each point to one another's beauty and majesty, seeking to glorify one another.

The Father glorifies His Son, Jesus, according to John 8:54: "Jesus replied, 'If I glorify myself, my glory means nothing. My Father, whom you claim as your God, is the one who glorifies me.'"

But Jesus also came to glorify the Father, as He said in John 17:4: "I [Jesus] have brought you glory on earth by completing the work you [the Father] gave me to do."

But that's not all. The Holy Spirit came to glorify Christ!

But when he, the Spirit of truth, comes, he will guide you into all truth. He will not speak on his own; he will speak only what he hears, and he will tell you what is yet to come. He will bring glory to me [Jesus] by taking from what is mine and making it known to you. (John 16:13-14)

Are you catching the beauty of all this? We're talking about God here! If anyone should have had the right to glorify themselves, it would have been Jesus and the Holy Spirit. But they didn't, and they don't. God is awesome glory clothed in beautiful humility.

The Lord Jesus, in fact, described Himself as being "gentle and humble in heart" (Matt. 11:29). Now you know someone is really humble when he *calls himself* "humble" and he is right! And Jesus is about the only person we know who can do that.

What about Us? _____

So where do we fit in? Well, as believers in Christ, we are to glorify God and not ourselves, as Paul clearly teaches in his first letter to the Corinthians:

> Do you not know that your body is a temple of the Holy Spirit who is in you, whom you have from God, and that you are not your own? For you have been bought with a price: therefore glorify God in your body. (1 Cor. 6:19–20 NASB)

Why should we bring glory to God? Because we belong to Him. He bought us out of horrible slavery to sin and Satan and has set us free to live a full and meaningful life here on Earth and in heaven. That should cause us to want to shout from the rooftops and praise His glorious name!

For some people, however, this is really tough. In fact, you might be saying right now, "What's the big idea with God wanting glory anyway? Is He on some kind of ego trip? Why should I glorify God when I've got nothing to live for? What did He ever do for me?"

We have spent thousands of hours with hurting people who desperately wish they could hear from God. To many of them, even the idea of doing God's will and glorifying Him is an unbearable burden. They feel like everyone else got the good stuff from God and all they got were the leftover scraps.

I (Neil) had the chance to meet with someone like that. He was a very successful man and a superintendent in a public school district. He went to church regularly and appeared pretty normal on the outside. But inside his mind there was a battle. He was driven by thoughts that constantly ordered him around. He had a hair-trigger temper as well as horrible nightmares that drained him of all energy.

Within a few hours of walking him through *The Steps to Freedom in Christ,* the man was free. Several months later, certain that what had happened was going to stick, the man wrote me a letter. Here is a part of it, slightly edited for clarity:

I never really understood the relationship God wanted to have with me. I saw God as an all-powerful but distant and stern father. Now I realize that God is like a real father in how He loves me. He wants me to enjoy His presence and live a fulfilling life on this earth. I used to see Him as a cold, disciplining God. I knew that I was to have a personal relationship with Him, but I had no way of knowing what that meant.

I compared my own dad's attitude toward a father/son relationship to the kind of friendship that I should have with God. I was dead wrong. God not only wants me to want to obey Him, but He also takes joy in my accomplishments.

I had struggled with my purpose in life. What did it matter if I achieved anything? If all my successes were the result of God's will, and all the glory belonged to Him, I thought that I must be just a worthless tool of the Almighty.

But I was wrong. There was no way I could be happy with this kind of belief. God wants me to do good things and take pleasure in doing them well. Just as an earthly father is pleased when his son does well, so too is God pleased when His children do His will.

I now have a new picture of God's love and my place in His plan. I have meaning, and what I do has meaning. I can take pleasure in doing good without risking the sin of pride. Now I see the truth—that God is a loving and caring Father. He gave me a will that I am supposed to use to please Him, and that is exactly what I intend to do.

What a difference the truth makes! It is the truth that sets us free (John 8:32) . . . free to love God and to *want* to glorify Him! Lies keep us in bondage, trapped in the web of Satan's deception. The devil wants us to see God as a selfish, power-hungry tyrant who needs His ego stroked. In reality, though, that is a good description of Satan himself, not God!

So how do we glorify God? Consider these Scriptures:

- Let your light shine before men in such a way that they may see your good works, and glorify your Father who is in heaven. (Matt. 5:16 NASB)
- If you abide in Me, and My words abide in you, ask whatever you wish, and it shall be done for you. By this is My Father glorified, that you bear much fruit, and so prove to be My disciples. (John 15:7-8 NASB)

How God Sees Us

People are struck by the greatness of God when He does things in and through our lives that only He can do. Answers to prayer. Areas of our lives changed by His power. Good works of love done in the wisdom and power of the Holy Spirit. Fellow students coming to Christ through your witness. All these things glorify God and cause people to praise and honor Him.

Our problem is that often we are stuck in our thinking. We don't see ourselves as God sees us. We think we are just the dirt under the toenail of the little toe of the body of Christ. And so we don't even bother to believe God could use us. Nothing could be further from the truth! We need to take a long, hard, and refreshing look at who we *really* are! Check out the words of Peter:

But you are a CHOSEN RACE, A ROYAL PRIESTHOOD, A HOLY NATION, A PEOPLE for God's OWN POSSESSION, *that you may proclaim the excellencies of Him who has called you out of darkness into His marvelous light; for you once were* NOT A PEOPLE, *but now you are* THE PEOPLE OF GOD; *you had* NOT RECEIVED MERCY, *but now you have* RECEIVED MERCY. *(1 Peter 2:9-10* NASB)

The world we live in sends us the message loud and clear: You are basically worth nothing unless you are beautiful, wealthy, handsome, popular, a star athlete, academic genius, or whatever. God sends us the message even louder and clearer: *You are of infinite value because I chose you and saved you and brought you into My family.* Believing what God says is true of you will make an awesome difference in how you live your life.

I (Neil) love the illustration in Bob George's *Classic Christianity.* Suppose you are a prostitute. One day you hear that all prostitutes are forgiven. Since you're a prostitute, that's great news! But would that news necessarily change how you behave or how you see yourself? Probably not.

You may dance in the streets for a while, but chances are you would be walking those streets by nightfall. You would see yourself as nothing more than a forgiven prostitute.

Now suppose the king not only forgave you, but he made you his bride as well. You're a queen! Would that change the way you live your life? You'd better believe it! Why would you want to live as a common prostitute if you were the queen?

You (along with all believers in Christ) are the bride of Christ. And that bride is the queen of the King of all kings and Lord of all lords! Regardless of how you may *feel*, that's who you really *are*!

You might be saying, "I would be filled with pride if I believed that!" Nonsense. You are who you are because of what *Christ* has done for you, not based upon any merit of your own. No, knowing the truth about who you are in Christ will set you free to live a victorious life. On the other hand, *not* believing the truths of who you are in Christ will leave you frustrated, discouraged, and defeated.

I (Rich) love thunderstorms. When I was a kid I would go out in the middle of them, watching the boiling clouds race by in the sky above me. Even if I was drenched with rain, I didn't care.

One day after a summer thunderstorm, I was walking down my driveway when I saw a butterfly. This one had obviously gotten its wings wet because it was walking along the ground instead of flying. It struck me as kind of funny—a butterfly that should be flying was crawling along the ground like a caterpillar!

Unfortunately, that's how most Christians live. They are new creatures in Christ—no longer sinners under God's judgment, but saints alive in Jesus! But they still act like the miserable sinners they used to be. They are like butterflies crawling along the ground as if they were still caterpillars.

Who You Really Are _____

The following is a list taken from Neil's book *Living Free in Christ*. It contains many of the things the Bible says are true of us because we are in Christ. They have nothing to do with how old you are or how long you've been a Christian. They have nothing to do with how mature you are as a believer in Jesus. They are as true for the baby believer as they are for Billy Graham.

Right now, this very moment, if you are God's child, God has already met your deepest needs for acceptance, security, and significance. Ask God to touch your heart with these wonderful truths from the Bible as you read them out loud. Then take time to look up the Scripture references in parentheses:

I am accepted *(Rom. 15:7)*.

I am God's child *(John 1:12-13)*.

I am Christ's friend *(John 15:12-17)*.

I have been justified *(Rom. 5:1)*.

I am united with the Lord and one with Him in Spirit *(1 Cor. 6:17)*.

I have been bought with a price; I belong to God *(1 Cor. 6:19-20)*.

I am a member of Christ's body *(1 Cor. 12:27)*.

I am a saint *(Eph. 1:1)*.

I have been adopted as God's child *(Eph. 1:5)*.

I have direct access to God through the Holy Spirit *(Eph. 2:17-18)*.

I have been redeemed and forgiven of all my sins *(Col. 1:13-14)*.

I am complete *(Col. 2:9-10)*.

I am secure *(Prov. 3:19-26)*.

I am free forever from condemnation *(Rom. 8:1-2)*.

I am assured that all things work together for good *(Rom. 8:28-30)*.

I am free from any condemning charges against me *(Rom. 8:31-34)*.

I cannot be separated from the love of God *(Rom. 8:35-39)*.

I have been established, anointed, and sealed by God *(2 Cor. 1:21-22)*.

I am hidden with Christ in God *(Col. 3:3)*.

I am confident that the good work God has begun in me will be perfected *(Phil. 1:6)*.

I am a citizen of heaven *(Phil. 3:20)*.

I have not been given a spirit of fear, but of power, love, and a sound mind *(2 Tim. 1:7)*.

I can find grace and mercy in time of need *(Heb. 4:16)*.

I am born of God and the evil one cannot touch me *(1 John 5:18-20)*.

I am significant *(1 Cor. 3:9; 4:1-2)*.

I am the salt of the earth and the light of the world *(Matt. 5:13-16)*.

I am a branch of the True Vine, a channel of His life *(John 15:1-5)*.

I have been chosen and appointed to bear fruit *(John 15:16-17)*.

I am a personal witness of Christ's *(Acts 1:8)*.

I am God's temple *(1 Cor. 3:16-17)*.

I am a minister of reconciliation *(2 Cor. 5:17-20)*.

I am God's coworker *(2 Cor. 6:1-2)*.

I am seated with Christ in the heavenly realm *(Eph. 2:6-7)*.

I am God's workmanship *(Eph. 2:10)*.

I may approach God with freedom and confidence *(Eph. 3:12)*.

I can do all things through Christ who strengthens me *(Phil. 4:11-13)*.[1]

Knowing who you are in Christ is one of the most important motivations for wanting to know and do the will of God. Listen to Paul's personal testimony: "But by the grace of God I am what I am, and his grace to me was not without effect. No, I worked harder than all of them—yet not I, but the grace of God that was with me" (1 Cor. 15:10).

A pastor's wife attended my (Neil) conference on "Resolving Personal and Spiritual Conflicts." She found out who she was as a child of God and found her freedom in Christ. She wrote, "I crave sharing Jesus with people out of my own love for Him, whereas before it was largely an 'I should' activity."

We are convinced that Christians will "work harder" when they understand what it means to be a child of God. But that hard work will no longer be in the energy of the flesh. It will be in the power of the Spirit of God! And that will bring great honor and glory to Him.

Only a child of God who knows who he or she is in Christ will be set free to live a life of joyful service to the glory of God. So let's stop trying to become something we already are!

We are children of God in Christ. In Him *we are* accepted unconditionally, loved perfectly, forgiven completely, and secure eternally.

Are you suffering today as a result of the sin of others? Are you caught in the consequences of your own bad choices? Have you thought that you were a helpless victim of your past? Have you fallen into the trap of blaming others, including God, for your spiritual struggles?

God offers freedom for hurting people. Today, will you begin to glorify Him and allow Him to show His glory in and through you as His precious son or daughter? If that is your heart's cry, would you join us as we pray?

Loving and merciful Father, open my eyes to see Your glory. Fill my heart with such a clear understanding of who You are and what You have done that I would want to shout it from the rooftops.

Please forgive me for the many times I have not glorified You but sought my own glory. Fill me with the Holy Spirit that I might bear much fruit and glorify You.

Thank You for giving me life and for adopting me as Your child. I want nothing else except for You to bring glory to Yourself through my life. You are the only One deserving of all honor, praise, and glory. I choose today to work by Your grace and power so that Your kingdom would come on earth as it has already come in heaven. In the gentle and humble name of Jesus I pray, amen.

God's Love Letter to You

What do all these things have in common: a light, a mirror, a sword, a hammer, rain, snow, milk, solid food, a belt, water, seed, fire? Give up? They are all word pictures that God uses to describe His Word, the Bible.

Let's look briefly at each of these terms and try to get the message the Lord wants to convey to us about the power of His Word and how it can help us know His will.

A *light* (Ps. 119:105) shines on the path we are taking to show us the way to go, protects us from stumbling over obstacles, keeps us from straying off the path and getting lost. God's Word is God's usual method of revealing His will. The Bible as light also dispels the darkness of fear and confusion so that we can walk confidently, hand in hand with God.

A *mirror* (James 1:23-25) shows us what we are like as

we look into it. When we read God's Word, we see in its pages an accurate reflection of who we are. We are children of God, loved and accepted completely as we are in Christ!

The mirror of God's Word also shows us when our attitudes or actions are not right. Then we must make adjustments based on what we have seen to be true about ourselves and not just walk away and forget what God has revealed.

A *sword* (Eph. 6:17) is our offensive weapon against the temptations, accusations, and deceptions of Satan. It is the spoken Word of God, the sword *of the Spirit*, and therefore must be used under His direction and in His power.

But this sword has a double edge. At times the Lord uses it like a scalpel, performing His gentle surgery on our hearts. The healing in our lives sometimes comes only when God uses His Word to cut out the impure motives and hidden sins in our hearts (Heb. 4:12-13).

A *hammer* (Jer. 23:29) is a tool God uses to "break a rock in pieces." Sometimes our hearts can grow cold, old, and moldy from unbelief and disobedience. God takes His Word and smashes the crusty hardness of our hearts in order to reveal Himself and show us His will.

Rain and snow (Isa. 55:10-11) provide essential moisture for living things to grow. God's Word, like the rain and snow, is sent by Him to help us grow up in our faith. It is powerful, refreshing, and life-giving, and it never fails to succeed in the matter for which God sends it.

Milk and solid food (Heb. 5:12-14) provide nourishment essential in helping human beings grow. Basic truths of the Christian faith are like milk for spiritual babies. It is what they need at that stage in life. They would choke on meat! The new Christian is told to crave God's Word like a newborn hungers for milk, since he or she has tasted that God is good (1 Peter 2:2-3).

Solid food refers to the deeper truths of God's Word that those who are more mature in Christ need. As we regularly feast on God's delicious health food (the Bible), chewing on what it says, it will give us great energy to know God and follow His will.

A *belt* (Eph. 6:14) is the truth that holds our spiritual "clothing" and "armor" in place. Since it is the truth that sets us free, we must daily put on that belt of truth to stand firm against the lies of Satan.

Jesus is the truth, and He holds all things together. He is the Word of God in human flesh. We must choose each day to "clothe ourselves with Christ" and make no provision for our flesh in regard to its lusts (Rom. 13:14).

Water (Eph. 5:26) is used for cleaning. God's Word is the purifying agent that the Spirit of God uses to wash our hearts clean of sin.

Seed (Luke 8:11) is the beginning of the planting of any crop. God wants to harvest a crop of right thinking and living in our lives. He plants the seed of His Word and over time it bears that crop. If, however, we allow the devil to have a place in our lives, he can cause us to forget that Word.

In addition, fear of what people think, the love of money, worries about the future, unhealthy relationships, and many other things can keep God's crop from bearing fruit. We must make the choice to say "no" to things that could cause our "noble and good heart" (Luke 8:15) to become hard toward God.

Fire (Jer. 23:29) is also used for purifying. Hot fire melts gold and causes the impurities (dross) to float to the surface where they can be skimmed off. The end product is a purer, more valuable gold than before. Like a hot fire, God's Word melts down areas of selfishness in our lives, so our faith becomes even more pure and precious in His sight.

It's a Love Letter _____

God could have chosen to leave us here on earth to fend

for ourselves. Instead, He wrote a love letter to every one of His children. We call it the Bible. In it God reveals Himself so we can get to know Him and His will.

It is easy, however, to bypass getting to know God in our eagerness to do what He wants. We must remember that the primary reason God gave us His Word is so that we could fall in love with Jesus. *God's Word* is meant to lead us to *God's Son*, as Jesus Himself told the religious leaders of His day: "You diligently study the Scriptures because you think that by them you possess eternal life. These are the Scriptures that testify about me, yet you refuse to come to me to have life" (John 5:39-40).

What was wrong with those Jewish leaders? Was Jesus mad at them for studying the Bible? No way! That was the one thing they were doing right. Their problem was that they stopped with the *words* of the Scriptures and missed the whole point of the words. What was the point? Jesus Himself.

Any study of God's Word in order to seek God's will is missing the point if it does not point us to a deeper love for and faith in Jesus.

How do you think I (Rich) would have felt if my little boy, Brian, at age one and a half, had come to me one day and said, "Daddy, would you write down on this piece of paper all the things you want me to do today? I want to make sure I obey you."

At first I would probably have had to pull myself up off the floor (especially since at that age he couldn't say much more than "Not me!" and "Daddy burped"). But assuming he was old enough to talk, I would be pretty happy. "The boy's finally learning some responsibility," I would probably say to myself.

But what if he did that every day? What if the only contact I had with him each day was for him to get my "to do" list?

I would very soon start to feel like our relationship was

empty. I would long to hold him and play with him. After about a day I would have to pull him up into my lap, hug him, and tell him what was *really* important to me: our relationship.

I want Brian to do what I say because he knows me, knows I love him, and knows I want nothing but the best for him. That's the way our heavenly Father wants us to come to His Word. Our problem, however, is that very often we have been duped by the devil into not spending time in the Bible at all. Or if we do read the Bible, it seems about as dry as Shredded Wheat in the desert with no milk.

From my years of working with youth, these are what I've found to be the most common complaints when it comes to spending time in God's Word:

- It's so boring! I don't get anything out of it.
- It's so big! I don't know where to start reading.
- It's so hard to concentrate! I find my mind wandering all over the place and sometimes I fall asleep.
- It's too hard to understand!

Chances are, if you have been a Christian for a while, you have experienced some or all of these problems. But not everyone feels this way about the Bible. Many times brand-new Christians dive into God's Word and have to practically be dragged away from it to come up for air! And even some mature Christian teens have developed a consistent, love relationship with God through His Word. What's their secret?

There's really no secret at all. God gave us in His Word some basic principles designed to enable us to get the most out of it.

The Way In _____

First, we need to admit our need for God's Word. When

Satan tempted Jesus to listen to His gut instead of His God, Jesus replied, "Man does not live on bread alone, but on every word that comes from the mouth of God" (Matt. 4:4).

How long would you have to go without food before your body began to let you know it was hungry? (For some of you guys, the answer to that question would be given in microseconds!) Somehow we all learn at an early age that our bodies need food. So do our souls. God's Word is the ultimate "soul food"!

Second, we need to realize that the devil is going to raise a fuss when we try to get into God's Word. Why is that? Jesus taught, "If you abide in My word, then you are truly disciples of Mine; and you shall know the truth, and the truth shall make you free" (John 8:31-32 NASB).

The devil wants to keep you on his leash to do his will. Jesus wants to set you free to do God's will. It shouldn't surprise us then to find ourselves in the middle of a battle.

The battle is for your mind. Our lives are changed by God through the renewing of our minds. Satan, the god of this world, wants to use the world around you to squeeze you into his mold (Rom. 12:1-2).

How do you win this battle? James 4:7 says, "Submit yourselves, then, to God. Resist the devil, and he will flee from you." How do you "submit" to God? Begin by asking the Lord to reveal to your mind the ways that you have grieved the Spirit of God and given access to the devil in your life. Confess any sin that He reveals to you, claiming God's forgiveness and cleansing based on 1 John 1:9. And if your mind is distracted by worries and concerns of the day, give each one to God in prayer. You can cast your anxiety on Him because He cares for you (1 Peter 5:7).

A thorough job of finding freedom in Christ is often necessary and always helpful in resisting the devil. We recommend that you walk through *The Steps to Freedom in Christ* (see the appendix) by yourself or with a trusted adult.

Third, pray before you read the Bible, and maintain an attitude of prayer as you read. Why? The Bible was written by God (through men), and only He can tell you what it really means and how He wants you to apply what it says. You will be amazed at the insights the Lord will give you about your life as you prayerfully read His Word! There is perhaps no more thrilling and yet humbling thing than to have the clear sense that God is speaking to you.

For example, my (Rich) wife, Shirley, and I had just gotten married. We were in the midst of some financial and health problems. I had the flu, and Shirley was getting over it. We were finally beginning to feel settled in our new apartment in the suburbs of Philadelphia. Shirley, having lived all her life in the South, was starting to adjust to life as a "Yankee."

The last thing on our minds was moving. Then a letter came from the leadership of our ministry. It asked us to consider moving to Manila, Philippines!

My first reaction was to groan and tell my wife, "No way! I've been to the Philippines. It is so hot and humid there. And Manila is crowded, dirty, and polluted. There's no way God is calling us to move there." Shirley's reaction was to cry. The prospect of moving again so soon was like a nightmare to her.

Over time, though, Shirley's heart began to change— much to my dismay! I didn't want to go (I love cold weather and snow), and I didn't want her to want to go either. But she started to get excited about the ministry opportunity. Deep down, I had to admit that it was a wonderful open door for God's work.

Our ministry leadership strongly yet lovingly urged us to prayerfully consider going. We had the qualifications needed and because we had no house or children, the move would be easier for us than for others.

Finally I came to the point of saying, "Father, not my will, but Thine be done." It was a battle to come to that point, there's no doubt about it. But it was the breakthrough the Lord was bringing about so that He could show me His will.

I went to His Word, asking Him to show me clearly if this was His will for us. I was reading prayerfully when I sensed a strong urging to turn to Matthew 28:18-20, the Great Commission. The words hit me in a new and fresh way: "Therefore go and make disciples of all nations."

The choice was mine. Would I go or stay?

"But, Lord," I protested, "I want to stay here in the U.S. and help bring revival to American students."

"Go," He repeated.

"But you created me to like the cold. I'm going to really suffer there in the tropics," I whined.

Then I had this vision in my mind of standing before the judgment seat of Christ, explaining to Him that the reason I didn't go to the Philippines was because I didn't like to sweat. Somehow I imagined that God would not be particularly impressed by my arguments.

He comforted me with those verses in Matthew 28, reminding me that He would be with me all the way.

All my defenses were finally down. I said, "Okay, Lord."

There is not space enough in this book to cover all the great things God did in and through us during our two-plus years in the Philippines.

Was it hard? Yes. Did I suffer? Yes, not only from the heat but from pneumonia and asthma (from the smog).

So was it really God's will? You better believe it! Are we glad we went? Absolutely. (And, to be perfectly honest, we're glad we're back too!)

Wasn't my desire to see revival come to American teenagers God's will for me? Yes, it was God's will, all right. But the timing wasn't right. He had some major surgery to do in my life before He would open that door. And His operating table happened to be in the Philippines.

God gave me direction through His Word to set me free to do His will. He wants to guide you too.

A fourth tip that will help you approach the Bible is to look at it as a bunch of little books joined together to make one big Book. Read one of the "little books" at a time and then move on to another. Don't let yourself be intimidated by its size. And don't feel like you have to start your reading in Genesis, although there is lots of good stuff in that book. God can speak to you on any page of His Word.

We suggest you start with one of the "little books" called the Gospels: Matthew, Mark, Luke, or John. Ask the Lord to open your eyes and heart to see Jesus as He really is. That is the Holy Spirit's job, according to John's gospel:

But when he, the Spirit of truth, comes, he will guide you into all truth. He will not speak on his own; he will speak only what he hears, and he will tell you what is yet to come. He will bring glory to me by taking from what is mine and making it known to you. (John 16:13-14)

Finally, go to God's Word with faith and anticipation. God loves you. He's got great things for you. He wants to speak to you. Don't be anxious, thinking you have to discover some great truth. Relax. The Spirit of God is perfectly willing and able to reveal to you what you need to see and know.

An incredible treasure of truth and love awaits you, as the apostle Paul declared in 1 Corinthians 2:9-10: "'No eye has seen, no ear has heard/no mind has conceived what God has prepared for those who love him'—but God has revealed it to us by his Spirit."

A growing knowledge of the Word of God is essential to

making wise decisions in the will of God. God's Word is filled with commands that we are to obey—these commands reveal clearly His will in many areas. These commandments are not meant to be heavy burdens (1 John 5:3). They have been given by our loving heavenly Father in order to protect us from what is harmful and to provide for us what is good.

Imagine that you and I are sheep, grazing on a beautiful, green pasture high on a plateau. We have lots of land on which we can roam and munch contentedly. Around the edge of this meadow, however, the shepherd has built a fence.

Curious as to what is beyond this barrier, we peer through the slats of the fence. There, on the other side, is a steep cliff, dropping off hundreds of feet. Only about five feet away, just out of our reach, is some really good-looking grass at the edge of the cliff. Though we strain and stretch, we can't quite reach it.

One of our friends, a ram, is determined to reach that delicious-looking grass. So he gets a running start, builds up a head of steam, and charges the fence. He hits it with such force that it buckles, and he plunges through . . . and down.

Was the shepherd being mean by building the fence? No, he was being loving. The ram learned that the hard way. In the same way, Jesus Christ, our Shepherd, sets limits for our lives. They are called "commands." Once we come to see that these limits are for our own good, life will be far easier for us.

God never directs us to take action contrary to what the Bible teaches. His Word *is* His will. For example, the Bible says that we should flee sexual immorality (1 Cor. 6:18). Why does He tell us to do this? Because our bodies are the temple of the Holy Spirit and we are to honor Him by what we do. No matter how much you and your boyfriend / girl-friend love each other, sexual intercourse before marriage is *never* God's will. It is simply always wrong, even if you "plan to marry" someday.

No matter how strong a desire you may have or how brilliant an idea may seem, if it violates a command or principle of God's Word, it is not from God. It's that simple. But obedience to God can sometimes be a lot easier said than done.

During my senior year in college, I (Rich) really wanted to be a witness for Christ in my major (meteorology). I was pumped. One day I caught wind of a seminar that one of my professors was conducting. In it he was going to try and describe how some miracles in the Bible could be explained scientifically as "optical illusions." The man had written a paper that suggested that the crossing of the Red Sea and Jesus' walk on the water could have been visual illusions.

Boy, was I ticked off! I really wanted to put this guy in his place for daring to even suggest that the Bible was not true! I tried to get a copy of his paper to study, but the only one I could find was on the desk of a graduate student.

I really felt like I needed to get my hands on that paper. I wanted to make sure my guns were loaded and ready. After all, the seminar was the next day! So I decided I should take the grad student's copy of the paper. "I'll just borrow it for a little while," I said to myself. "How else can I prepare?"

Fortunately, some older and more mature believers stopped me cold. "That would be stealing," they said. I protested, saying that I could leave a little note on his desk. "But what if he needs it?" they argued. "I'll only keep it for a short time," I explained.

Thank God I finally listened to my brothers in Christ, or a really nasty scandal could have occurred. I would have been guilty of breaking the law of God in the name of doing the will of God!

The *command* of the Bible was obvious: "Thou shalt not steal." Taking something that does not belong to you is wrong, pure and simple. But the *principle* of God's Word that I violated was not so obvious. What had my attitude been? To really *get* that professor. First Peter 3:15 instructs us, however, to give a defense for the Christian faith "with gentleness and reverence" (NASB).

I believe that my attitude of anger and resentment toward the professor had opened a door in my life for the devil to deceive me (Eph. 4:26-27) into thinking that taking the paper would have been for "a good cause."

An Essential Lesson

There is one more critical lesson to be learned from my blunder: It is very easy to become so excited about an idea, impression, dream, or goal that we lose touch with the direction of God and His will. In those highly energized, emotional states of mind, we can come up with a million and one reasons why a certain Bible verse doesn't apply to us. Beware! At times like these you will not likely be able to discern God's will on your own. You will need to go to a wiser, more mature believer in Christ (who is not emotionally involved) for advice. He or she may be able to protect you from great error.

Do not, however, become lazy. This is not a license to neglect personal Bible study. Each one of us has the responsibility to learn how to study God's Word ourselves and interpret it correctly, as 2 Timothy 2:15 clearly tells us: "Be diligent to present yourself approved to God as a workman who does not need to be ashamed, handling accurately the word of truth" (NASB).

Be very careful as well about reading the Bible in the hope that a certain verse or word will "jump out" at you. Make sure that what you think the Bible is saying lines up with the entire teaching of the Scriptures. An isolated word, phrase, or sentence taken out of its context can appear to say something entirely different from what God intended it to say.

Remember, even the devil tried to use the Word of God to tempt Jesus in the wilderness. Matthew recorded that incident in the fourth chapter of his gospel:

> *Then the devil took him [Jesus] to the holy city and had him stand on the highest point of the temple. "If you are the Son of God," he said, "throw yourself down. For it is written:*
>
> > *'He will command his angels concerning you,*
> > *and they will lift you up in their hands,*
> > *so that you will not strike your foot against a stone.'"*
>
> *Jesus answered him, "It is also written: 'Do not put the Lord your God to the test.'" (Matt. 4:5-7)*

Satan knows the Word of God backward and forward, and he'll try to use it for his advantage. In this case he quoted Psalm 91:11-12, but he took it out of context, twisting its intended meaning and using it as a tool of temptation. Jesus never even blinked an eye. He quoted Deuteronomy 6:16 correctly and put the devil in his place.

If you are ever confused about what God's Word is saying about God's will, ask the Lord for wisdom. If two Scriptures seem to contradict one another, you are interpreting at least one of them incorrectly. You may need to talk with your parents or pastor to solve your dilemma.

Again, let us encourage you to relax and enjoy your reading of God's Word. It is the primary avenue by which your loving, heavenly Father reveals Himself and His will.

Don't go off the deep end trying to find Bible verses to answer questions such as whether you should brush your teeth or use your deodorant first in the morning. God doesn't care in which order you do them, just so you do them (Matt. 7:12)! Some things simply don't matter. Others require simple common sense. Use your head!

The devil wants us to get hung up on trivial pursuits. God wants us to walk with Him through the pages of His Word, growing in our love for Him and in our ability to listen to the Shepherd's voice. The apostle Paul's prayer for the Colossian believers hits the nail right on the head:

> *For this reason, since the day we heard about you, we have not stopped praying for you and asking God to fill you with the knowledge of his will through all spiritual wisdom and understanding. And we pray this in order that you may live a life worthy of the Lord and may please him in every way: bearing fruit in every good work, growing in the knowledge of God, being strengthened with all power according to his glorious might so that you may have great endurance and patience, and joyfully giving thanks to the Father, who has qualified you to share in the inheritance of the saints in the kingdom of light. (Col. 1:9-12)*

Does Paul's prayer express your heart's desire? It is primarily through the Word of God that He will answer that prayer.

> *Dear heavenly Father, Your Word is truth. It is living and active, sharper than any two-edged sword. You use it to judge the thoughts and motivations of my heart so that I might know You and Your pure will. You use it to shred the devil's lies.*
> *Thank You that the Bible is inspired by You and useful for teaching me what I need to know, for showing me where I am wrong, for correcting me, and for training me to live in the right way.*
> *Help me to see Your Word as a personal love letter from You to me. Fill my heart with a longing to hear*

Your gentle, quiet voice leading me through its pages. Teach me Your will by the Spirit of truth as I read the Bible, and please protect my mind from self-deception and all the tricks of the enemy. I commit myself to do Your will alone. In Jesus' name, amen.

A
Peace
of My Mind

Sleep in heavenly peace. The words of the carol, "Silent Night," were an inviting offer to my (Rich) weary body at 1 A.M. Christmas Eve. I had just finished unsuccessfully trying to fix a part of my daughter's "big gift"—a plastic kitchen stove complete with telephone! Something of the simple joy of that first Christmas seemed to get lost in the middle of my frenzied hammering and frustrated grumbling.

I often wonder how we have managed in this country to become so busy. Is "busyness" next to godliness? You would think so, the way Christians boast about their exhausting schedules. Have peace and quiet in our lives and hearts become swallowed up in action and activity? Have we lost our ability to "be still and know that I am God" (Ps.

46:10)? For many of us—even sincere Christians—I am afraid that is the case. We have been seduced by the spirit of the age that says we cannot be happy or comfortable unless we are doing something.

If things continue on the present course and Christian parents and young people do not wake up, we could very well see a whole generation gripped by an epidemic of burnout. Violence, drug abuse, alcoholism, suicide, and a whole plague of mental and emotional disorders will result if we fail to learn that "in repentance and rest is your salvation, in quietness and trust is your strength" (Isa. 30:15).

The problem, though, goes beyond hyper-busyness. Busyness is often merely a symptom of a deeper problem—a restless heart driven to activity by that cruel taskmaster, anxiety, or a lack of *peace*.

That Wonderful Word

There are three kinds of peace described in the Bible: peace with God, peace on earth, and the peace of God.

The first one, *peace with God*, already belongs to every Christian. Though we were once at war with God and were, in fact, His enemies, that has been resolved. Listen to the words of Paul, the former enemy of Jesus Christ:

> *Therefore having been justified [declared not guilty] by faith, we have peace with God through our Lord Jesus Christ. . . . For if while we were enemies, we were reconciled to God through the death of His Son, much more, having been reconciled, we shall be saved by His life. (Rom. 5:1, 10 NASB)*

The war is over! It's a done deal. In Christ we have waved the white flag and surrendered to our conquering King Jesus. But we are not prisoners of war waiting to be tried in the Heavenly Court of Justice. We are now friends, eternally at peace with God through what Christ has done for us.

If you struggle with a nagging anxiety that God is one day going to turn on you, take heart! Romans 8:1 says, "There is therefore now no condemnation for those who are in Christ Jesus" (NASB).

Believe it! If you are a Christian, you *have* peace with God!

The second kind of peace, *peace on earth*, is something we look forward to when Jesus Christ reigns on earth as Prince of Peace. Until then, unfortunately, wars will remain a horrible reality of life.

It is the last "peace issue" that we want to focus on in the remainder of this chapter, because this is an important part of God's will for our lives.

God's Remedy

Peace. It is God's remedy for a world gone crazy. It is living life in the eye of the storm where gentle breezes bathe our spirits while a hurricane of hurry and worry rages around us. It is God's "Secret Service," guarding our hearts and minds in Christ Jesus (Phil. 4:6-7).

When we talk about experiencing the *peace of God*, we are not talking about the absence of conflict or problems. We are talking about experiencing peace in the midst of trials . . . a peace that too often exits with the first sign of trouble. This unrest in our souls comes from believing several devastating lies about God and His will.

The first area of anxiety comes from believing the lie that it is more important to *serve God* than to *seek God*. In Luke's gospel we find a story of two sisters who learned what was really important to Jesus:

As Jesus and his disciples were on their way, he came to a vil-

*lage where a woman named Martha opened her home to
him. She had a sister called Mary, who sat at the Lord's feet
listening to what he said. But Martha was distracted by all
the preparations that had to be made. She came to him and
asked, "Lord, don't you care that my sister has left me to do
the work by myself? Tell her to help me!"*

*"Martha, Martha," the Lord answered, "you are worried
and upset about many things, but only one thing is needed.
Mary has chosen what is better, and it will not be taken
away from her." (Luke 10:38-42)*

Is it wrong to serve Christ? Of course not! . . . unless it
robs us of our intimate fellowship with the Lord. For Jesus
said that seeking Him was more important than serving
Him. Our service *for* Christ is meant to be an outflow of
our relationship *with* Christ!

Don't let yourself get faked out. First, learn to spend
quiet, unhurried time in the presence of God—in the Bible
and prayer. He will draw you close to Himself and *He* will
show you how to serve Him. God is not pleased by our
self-directed efforts to do what we presume to be His will.
You can rest peacefully, knowing that He will guide you as
you wait for His leading.

Maybe God has led you into a very busy lifestyle. If so,
you need to make sure that though your schedule is like
Martha's, your heart is like Mary's!

The next area of anxiety comes from believing the lie that
happiness and success come from the accumulation of
things. Jesus knew that we would struggle with this one, so
He laid it on the line in Matthew 6:

*Do not store up for yourselves treasures on earth, where
moth and rust destroy, and where thieves break in and steal.
But store up for yourselves treasures in heaven, where moth
and rust do not destroy, and where thieves do not break in*

*and steal. For where your treasure is, there your heart will
be also. (Matt. 6:19-21)*

If you believe you need certain kinds of clothes, computer
equipment, stereos, cars, houses, and vacations to bring you
happiness, then you will work like crazy to get those things,
and you will be anxious until you get them—and you will
have no peace.

"Will I do well enough in school to get into the right
college? Will I do well enough in college to get the right job?
Will I land the right job so I can get the right salary?" And
on and on.

The Caution Light Is Blinking

The materialistic treadmill never stops. Once you get
what you want, something even better will come along and
you will be anxious until you get that too. And with
increased wealth comes the increased anxiety over high
repair costs and elaborate means of providing security for
your possessions.

In the end, you won't end up possessing your toys. They
will possess you.

You need to choose this day whom you will serve (Josh.
24:15). As usual, Jesus pulled no punches as He continued
His preaching about money: "No one can serve two masters. Either he will hate the one and love the other, or he
will be devoted to the one and despise the other. You cannot
serve both God and Money" (Matt. 6:24).

The choice is yours: Either believe that God will ultimately take care of you and your future needs, or believe
that your pursuit of Money will provide you with the
security and pleasure you desire. But there is no middle
ground here. Jesus said it Himself: You simply can't serve
two masters. There are no exceptions to the rule.

The way of Jesus is a way of peace, not anxiety, focusing on the present (Matt. 6:25-32). Realize that your Father in heaven who takes care of the plants and animals around you can be trusted to take care of your future. Why? Because we are far more valuable to Him than birds and flowers are. Remember, God loves *you!* And once you begin living that truth, you will experience the peace of God. Jesus summed it up this way:

Seek first his [God's] kingdom and his righteousness, and all these things [that we need in life] will be given to you as well. Therefore do not worry about tomorrow, for tomorrow will worry about itself. Each day has enough trouble of its own. (Matt. 6:33-34)

An Incredible Story

Several years ago, a close friend of ours was in a morning prayer meeting when he felt strongly impressed from the Lord to pray for his wife. As he was saying "amen," he received a message on his beeper to call home.

Minutes before, his wife had been awakened by a knock at their door. Some painters (at least one of whom was a Christian) had decided at the last minute to drop off some paint to the house next door, even though they were not going to start the job till the next day. The painters had spotted a fire. It had started when a windstorm blew a power line into a dried palm branch next to our friend's house. The fire had quickly spread to our friends' roof, unknown to the sleeping woman ... until the painters had knocked on her door.

The house was destroyed and most of their possessions damaged beyond recovery, but the two of them were safe.

In a matter of months our friends were able to move into a beautiful new home—the insurance company had replaced everything. It was like a dream come true as they were allowed to choose the colors for the paint, drapes, and carpet. They were living witnesses of the truth that God "is able to do exceeding abundantly beyond all that we ask or think" (Eph. 3:20 NASB)!

Through all that this couple had endured, they were an incredible example of this truth: "He [God] will keep in perfect peace all those who trust in him, whose thoughts turn often to the Lord! Trust in the Lord God always, for in the Lord Jehovah is your everlasting strength" (Isa. 26:3-4 TLB).

But that is not the end of the story. I (Rich) just hung up the phone after hearing more sad news about these two godly servants of the Lord.

Just prior to Christmas, their joy turned to heartache as they lost their second child in a miscarriage. (Even the word sounds so cold.) A human life, so precious to this couple to whom pregnancy had come with difficulty, was gone. The child went safely into the everlasting arms of our Father in heaven, to be sure, but a grieving emptiness still fills our friends' souls.

Is it still possible for this couple to walk in peace? Will anxiety overtake them and gnaw at their hearts as they think about future pregnancies?

That is still not the end of the story. After a week of Christmas vacation away from home with family, they returned to find their house closed up by the police. While they were gone, a group of drug dealers had broken into their home and turned it into a lab for making methamphetamine (speed). The intruders had stolen most of their valuables, but that wasn't the worst of it. During their stay there, some methane gas had exploded, totaling the house. What wasn't destroyed in the blast was contaminated by the poisonous gas released in the explosion. Basically, all their earthly possessions were gone again.

Few people lose everything. For this couple, it has happened twice in two years!

How is peace of mind and peace of heart possible when all hell seems to break loose on us? It's a matter of where your treasure (what you value most) really is, because Jesus said that "where your treasure is, there your heart will be also" (Matt. 6:21).

For Roger and Debbie McNichols, there is a powerful and deep peace guarding their hearts and minds this day. This is the peace of God. It did not come without a battle with anger, depression, and anxiety. But it came. Why? Because fire, thieves, and an explosion may have destroyed their possessions, but those things never touched their true treasure.

What they value most—entering into the joy of their Master, and enjoying the rewards of serving their Lord Jesus Christ—awaits them in heaven, safe and sound. They rest secure in the arms of their heavenly Father.

So what do you do when anxiety locks its unnerving grip on your soul, draining you of peace and strength? Philippians 4:6-9 gives the cure:

> *Do not be anxious about anything, but in everything, by prayer and petition, with thanksgiving, present your requests to God. And the peace of God, which transcends all understanding, will guard your hearts and your minds in Christ Jesus.*
> *Finally, brothers, whatever is true, whatever is noble, whatever is right, whatever is pure, whatever is lovely, whatever is admirable—if anything is excellent or praiseworthy—think about such things. Whatever you have learned or received or heard from me, or seen in me—put it into practice. And the God of peace will be with you.*

Prescription for Worried Minds _____

Did you get it? If not, here's the prescription for anxiety relief that God wrote out for us:

Dump the whole deal on God in prayer. Tell Him what's got you worried. Peter put it this way: "Cast all your anxiety on him [God] because he cares for you" (1 Peter 5:7). God really cares, so no matter how big or small your concern is, you can tell Him!

Thank God that He cares and that He is in control. Thanking Him demonstrates faith and will remind you that God is big enough to handle your problems. Much anxiety comes from a false belief that we have to control what goes on around us—people, circumstances, our future. No! Our times are in God's hands (Ps. 31:15).

Choose to focus your thoughts on true and good things. These are things like God's love, power, and wisdom. Refuse to dwell on negative thoughts that could throw you back into a tailspin of worry or fear. If necessary, take out a piece of paper and divide it into two columns. On the left, write down the things you *know* to be true. On the right, write down the things you *think* or *feel* might be true. We call those "speculations." Pray and ask God to help you separate *truth* from mere *speculation.* Our imaginations tend to create "worse-case scenarios" in our minds—use discipline to concentrate on the things that are true.

Make the choice to live responsibly. Do what you can according to the instructions of Scripture. Seek to be a peacemaker, if a relationship is not as it should be (Matt. 5:9). "If it is possible, as far as it depends on you, live at peace with everyone" (Rom. 12:18). Forgive others who have hurt you and do not take revenge. Seek to overcome the evil that was done to you by doing good in return (Rom. 12:19-21).

(Recognize, however, that even after you have done everything, others may still refuse to apologize or be friends with you. Again, don't try to control others. Leave them to God. The fruit of the Spirit is "self-control"—not parent-control or brother/sister-control or friend-control. It is not even boyfriend- or girlfriend-control!)

After you faithfully follow this fourfold plan, what will result? Will everyone and everything around you be as you would like it to be? Not necessarily. But everything *within* you will be as you need it.

You will experience the peace of God. That peace will protect you from going crazy. It will settle your soul so you can discern God's leading again and walk in peaceful wisdom and righteousness. And not only that, but the God of peace Himself will be with you. And when all is said and done, that is really all you need anyway, isn't it? Will you join us in prayer?

Dear heavenly Father, I confess to You that many times I have tried to control my own life, and because of that I have been robbed of Your peace. I choose today to make You my Master and to trust You to provide all I need for the present and the future. I cast any and every anxiety on You, because You really do care for me. I choose to quiet my heart before You. I want to be still and know that You are God.
I choose today to put seeking You even above serving You, and I ask for Your daily guidance. I give up any efforts to control other people or circumstances, and I choose today to let Your Spirit develop self-control in me. I joyfully acknowledge that You are in control and I am not, and I thank You for being trustworthy. Fill me now with Your Spirit so that I can experience the peace that comes from resting in You. Amen.

Uncommon Sense

A sincere Christian man was listening to his radio one day when an urgent warning came over the airwaves. The peaceful valley in which he lived was under a flash flood warning! Immediately the man fell to his knees and prayed that God would rescue him.

Those words were still on his lips when he turned to see the floodwaters gushing under his door. He raced up the stairs to the second floor of his house and climbed out onto the roof.

Not long after, a helicopter flew by and the pilot asked over the loudspeaker if he could airlift him off.

"That's not necessary, since I have the Lord's protection," the man replied.

Moments later the house began to break apart, and the

man found himself swept downstream. Fortunately, he was able to cling to a tree for safety. A police boat, braving the waters, approached him for a rescue. The Christian man assured them, however, that the Lord would save him.

Finally, the tree gave way, and the man was unable to fight the rampaging current. He drowned.

Standing before the Lord, he asked, "Lord, I'm glad to be here, but why didn't You answer my prayer for safety?"

The Lord responded, "Son, I did answer your prayer. First, I told you over the radio to get out of there. Then I sent you a helicopter and a police rescue boat, but you still wouldn't go!"

Silly story, right? Maybe so, but it has a point: When you pray, expect God to answer—but don't suppose that God only works through extraordinary means. Most often He operates supernaturally through very ordinary means.

Sometimes we can miss God's guidance because we are looking for some spectacular event. He can certainly work that way, because "Our God is in heaven; he does whatever pleases him" (Ps. 115:3). We set ourselves up for frustration, however, when we think God *has* to work that way all the time.

Some Christians *always* look for a sign or wonder as the only confirmation that God is working or guiding. But we need to be careful not to put God in a box . . . even a miraculous one. Jesus sternly rebuked those who always sought a miraculous sign from Him. Read carefully:

Then some of the scribes and Pharisees answered Him, saying, "Teacher, we want to see a sign from You." But He answered and said to them, "An evil and adulterous generation craves for a sign; and yet no sign shall be given to it but the sign of Jonah the prophet." (Matt. 12:38-39 NASB)

Jesus was right. We dare not put God into a position

where He is forced to prove His love or power to us. It is sin to try to back God into that kind of corner. When God wishes to do the miraculous, He will do it of His own free will. Actually, it should give us a sense of security to know that God very often guides us through the simple, everyday people and events of life. After all, most of life is well, pretty ordinary, wouldn't you say?

The Keys: Dependence and Faith _____

In His Word, God has revealed much of Himself and many of His ways to us. Yet many decisions we need to make in life are not spelled out in the Bible. How do we discern God's will in those cases? The bottom line is that we must develop a heart of dependence upon God. Just because God may use ordinary means to direct our steps doesn't mean we are any less dependent on Him to guide us! Proverbs 3:5-7 shows us clearly what kind of relationship God desires to have with us:

> Trust in the LORD with all your heart
> and lean not on your own understanding;
> in all your ways acknowledge him,
> and he will make your paths straight.
> Do not be wise in your own eyes;
> fear the LORD and shun evil.

It is easy to assume we know what's best for ourselves, because we know what we like and what we want. But true wisdom is seeing life from God's point of view, not our own. When we are wise in our own eyes, we are sure to become blinded to God's path for our lives.

How do you demonstrate your trust in God rather than yourself? Your prayer life will show the level of your trust. The one who says he is leaning on God will keep the communication lines continually open between him and his heavenly Father. And he will be looking for God's answer, because he knows God delights in responding to the prayers of His children.

As I (Rich) approached my college graduation, I had a major decision to make. Even though I enjoyed forecasting the weather (my major in college), I just couldn't see myself doing that the rest of my life. What I really wanted to do was something that would affect people's lives for eternity. There was no doubt in my mind that God had changed my desires and wanted me to go into full-time Christian service.

At that time, my exposure to Christian ministries was very limited. I was familiar with the ministry of Campus Crusade for Christ from college, and I knew about seminaries. So, I figured God either wanted me to go on full-time staff with Campus Crusade or attend seminary. In order to find out which one He wanted, I attended a weekend conference on knowing the will of God. I prayed that God would show me His will during those two days. I had tried and tried to decide on my own, but I just couldn't figure out which one was best for me. They both seemed equally good.

Ray was one of the first men I met at the conference. He was an older man who impressed me with his gentle, wise spirit. I told him about my dilemma and asked if he had any thoughts. Interestingly enough, Ray was at that time on the staff of Campus Crusade and had also graduated from seminary!

I couldn't believe it! God had led me to somebody who had experience in the exact areas in which I was interested. By asking me a few questions, Ray realized I hadn't had much ministry experience.

He suggested that I serve with Campus Crusade for a few years to gain more practical ministry training. Then I could still attend seminary if I wanted to. He felt that experience with Campus Crusade would best prepare me to understand

and apply the knowledge I would gain in seminary, if I ever attended one.

Now, that is certainly not going to be God's plan for everyone, but for me, it was the wisest advice. I stayed on staff with Campus Crusade for seventeen years!

The keys to having God's wisdom in a matter are *dependence* and *faith*. Dependence says, "I choose to rely on God to show me His ways rather than relying on my own ability to figure things out." Faith says, "I expect God to answer my prayer for guidance, and I will keep looking toward Him to see how He will direct me."

For the rest of this chapter, we'll look at seven ways in which Christians commonly seek God's guidance. Then we'll conclude by listing ten factors that will help lead you toward a wise decision. If you have read this far in the book, most likely you are sincerely seeking God and His ways. He will not disappoint you.

Seven Avenues for God's Guidance

Conscience. Should you "let your conscience be your guide"? That can be tricky. Your conscience is that part of your mind that tries to tell you what is right and wrong. But before you became a Christian, your mind was set on the flesh and programmed (at least in part) by the world. So your conscience is not always reliable.

Many people struggle with a guilty conscience. They may feel guilty for saying "no" to someone, even though it is the right thing to do. This false guilt can drive a people-pleaser to do what people want rather than what God wants. Paul said, "If I were still striving to please men, I would not be a bond-servant of Christ" (Gal. 1:10 NASB).

It is also possible to dull the voice of our conscience through repeated acts of immorality. The Bible calls this a "seared conscience" (1 Tim. 4:2). We are instructed in

God's Word, to keep a "clear conscience" and to strive to maintain a "good conscience" (1 Peter 3:16, 21).

How do we do this? By renewing our minds with God's Word so that our conscience adopts God's standards of right and wrong. Recognize, then, that the Holy Spirit will work through your conscience. Be very cautious about going against your own conscience once you are committed to Christ.

We are, however, to restrict our freedom (even if our conscience says that something is okay), if it causes a weaker brother to stumble in his faith. We never have the right to violate another person's conscience. "Let us therefore make every effort to do what leads to peace and to mutual edification" (Rom. 14:19).

Fleeces. In Judges 6, Gideon was called by God to deliver Israel from the Mideonites. But Gideon had some real problems believing God could use him, so he asked God for a sign. God gave him one, but Gideon was still not sure, so he tried an experiment.

He put a lamb's fleece on the ground. According to Gideon's prayer, if the fleece was wet with dew in the morning and the ground was dry, God would indeed deliver Israel. When Gideon checked the fleece the next morning, that's what he found! But was that good enough for him? No way.

Wanting to be sure, and hoping that God would not get too mad, Gideon asked God to do it again. But this time, he wanted the ground to be wet and the fleece to be dry. *Voilà!* God came through again!

Even though God mercifully granted his requests, Gideon was not demonstrating faith by putting out the fleeces. God had already told him clearly, prior to his "sheepish" experiments, that He would deliver Israel through Gideon (Judg. 6:14-16). Beware of putting out "fleeces" to confirm God's will when He has already spoken clearly in His Word. You could easily be deceived by your own flesh or the devil. What are some examples of fleeces?

- "Well, if my youth pastor is at the local convenience store when I go there, I won't buy the *Playboy* magazine."
- "I'll do my homework if my favorite TV shows are canceled tonight."
- "I'll get serious about You, Lord, if my girlfriend/boyfriend becomes a Christian."

We need no more confirmation once God has spoken through His Word. It is risky business to play fleecing games with God. Remember, "Do not be deceived: God cannot be mocked. A man reaps what he sows" (Gal. 6:7).

Circumstances. Some of us assume that God reveals His will through circumstances. If they look good, it's God's will; if they don't, it isn't. Next to the Bible, probably more Christians make decisions by this means than by any other. Yet circumstances can be very unreliable.

Many times we give up on something just because things are tough at first. Remember that we have an enemy who will try to thwart the working of God every step of the way. We need to learn to persevere in prayer and learn to be content in whatever circumstance we are in (Phil. 4:11).

Circumstances can be helpful, however, in determining the *timing* of God's will. When we ask God for something, He may answer, "Yes, right away," or "No, that's not good for you," or "Yes, but not right now." Many times God wants us to wait a while because we or someone else is not yet ready for what He wishes to give. Learning to wait for God's timing is perhaps one of the hardest things in life to do, but the results can be quite sweet!

When I (Rich) first sought to have my book *To My Dear Slimeball* published, I wrote to thirty-one different Christian publishing houses. Most never wrote back. A few asked for a couple of chapters of the book. One even invited me to the office for an interview. But in the end, no one accepted the book.

Finally, months later, a publisher did accept it. (It turned out to be one of those that had initially rejected it!) I had to wait nearly three years from the time I first started writing the book until it was released. Was it hard? That's an understatement! It was agonizing at times! But God was (and still is!) teaching me to wait for His perfect timing. And when His timing is fulfilled . . . how sweet it is! When I finally saw the finished product, I felt a deep satisfaction—far more than if the book had come out earlier. Why? Because I had hung in there with the book—writing, rewriting, and rewriting again, until it was the way God wanted it.

Parents and Godly Counsel. Proverbs 13:10 says, "Pride only breeds quarrels, but wisdom is found in those who take advice." Sound familiar? How many times have you gotten into an argument with your parents over some part of your life (e.g., your friends, your music, your household chores) because you didn't want to listen to what they had to say?

God has provided your parents as a primary means of showing you His will. Unless they are asking you to do something contrary to the clear teaching of the Bible, you are smart to follow what they say. Check out what Paul said to the kids and teens in Ephesus:

Children, obey your parents in the Lord, for this is right. "Honor your father and your mother"—which is the first commandment with a promise—"that it may go well with you and that you may enjoy long life on the earth." (Eph. 6:1-3)

We know your parents aren't perfect, and sometimes they

don't seem to be willing to listen to your side of the story. In cases like that you may have to bite your tongue and be "quick to listen, slow to speak and slow to become angry." Your angry outbursts will not bring about God's will (James 1:19-20).

In things related to your Christian life, you can also seek out godly counsel from your pastor, youth pastor, and other older, more mature believers. This is especially important if your parents are not Christians. But don't look for people you know will just agree with you. That's neither a sign of wisdom nor maturity.

Weigh any advice you receive carefully. People may give you counsel out of selfish motives. It is best to get advice from individuals who know the Word of God, who are sensitive to the Spirit of God, and who are not going to be swayed by personal biases.

Gifts and Abilities. After I (Neil) taught a class on spiritual gifts, a young man came to me and asked, "Is my gift prophecy or exhortation?" Knowing him very well, I was careful as I responded. "I don't think either one is your gift," I began. "But if I have ever known someone who has the gift of helps, you're it. You're sensitive to the needs of other people and always ready to help."

A look of disappointment came over his face. "I knew it!" he responded. Struggling with low self-esteem, he was pursuing what he wrongly perceived to be a greater gift.

Our sense of self-worth isn't to be based on what gift we have. Our self-acceptance comes from who we are in Christ (our identity) and who we are becoming in Christ (our character). Any teenager who understands who he or she is as a child of God and whose life shows the fruit of the Spirit will have a healthy self-image.

God knows us perfectly. He created us. And He has given each of us certain abilities. His will always includes the expression of those abilities. You can be sure that He will lead you in such a way that makes the best use of the gifts and talents He has given you!

It is our responsibility to take full advantage of the opportunities that arrive to develop and use those God-given gifts for His glory. Tragically, many people go to the grave with their music still in them, never contributing to the symphony of God's work.

Don't be afraid to take risks. God surely wants you to use the abilities He has given you. Ask Him to guide you, and don't be surprised if He directs you to do something beyond your comfort zone. Don't make the mistake of clinging to the security of the tree trunk when the fruit is always out on the end of the limb!

Duty. Do you know how much of our Christian life is simply a matter of duty and responsibility? Most of it. You don't need God to tell you to live a responsible life.

For example, you don't need to pray to find out whether God wants you to finish high school or clean up your room or do your homework or help out with the chores around the house. You already know those things are the right things to do.

There are a lot of days when I (Rich) don't feel like getting up or changing diapers or washing dishes or doing paper-work. At that moment I certainly don't feel any special "leading" to do so. If I relied on my feelings, I would be in trouble . . . especially from my wife!

Sometimes we can come up with all kinds of excuses for not doing what, deep down, we know we should do. We are wise to listen to James's strong reminder, "Anyone, then, who knows the good he ought to do and doesn't do it, sins" (James 4:17).

Desires. King David wrote, "Delight yourself in the LORD and he will give you the desires of your heart" (Ps. 37:4). I can see it now—every teenager reading this book is starting to drool over the new Corvette, Mustang, or Porsche that

God is going to give him or her! Sorry to disappoint you, gang.

The key to that Scripture is that we delight ourselves *in the Lord*. If you do, your desires will begin to change. You will start to want the things that He wants. Your heart will become filled with the things that are on His heart.

Unfortunately, many of us delight ourselves *in the desires of our heart* rather than in the Lord! That is the surefire way to frustration. As Christians we constantly have a battle going on inside of us. It is the struggle between the desires of the flesh and those of the Spirit—between our own selfish desires and God's holy will.

Jesus said, "Blessed [truly happy] are those who hunger and thirst for righteousness, for they shall be satisfied" (Matt. 5:6 NASB). Do you believe that is true? If you do, you will demonstrate that belief by living according to the Spirit.

We guarantee, however, that if you try to satisfy the desires of the flesh, you will never succeed. The more you feed the flesh, the hungrier it gets. The only way to keep your selfish lusts of the flesh in line is to walk by the power of the Holy Spirit.

In determining God's will for your life, then, the crucial question is this: Do you intend to live according to the flesh or the Spirit?

The Wisdom Checklist _____

We have provided a checklist at the end of this chapter to help when you are faced with a decision. We will discuss each of the ten questions briefly here.

First, *Have you prayed about it?* Prayer shows that you want and need God's will. It was never intended to be a "fourth-down, punting situation" in which we finally ask God to bail us out. Prayer is meant to be the "first play called in the huddle."

God does not want us to make all our plans and decisions and *then* ask Him to bless them! He wants us to seek Him first and find out what His plans are!

God could have decided to just give us everything we need, but He has taught us to pray, "Give us this day our daily bread." We are dependent upon God, and prayer is the evidence that we realize our need for Him. It is easy to try all our own ideas first and if nothing else works, then pray. But we are told to "seek *first* the kingdom of God" (Matt. 6:33 NKJV).

Second, *Is it consistent with the Word of God?* When in doubt, check it out! Ask God to direct you in His Word. If you are clueless about where to look, talk to your parents (if they are believers), youth leader, pastor, or mature Christian friends. Or go to a local Christian bookstore if necessary and ask the manager to suggest a book on the topic.

Also, learn how to use a concordance (check out your Bible—it might even have a short one in the back). A concordance lists the Bible verses that include a particular word, such as *patience* or *righteousness*. Since it is arranged in alphabetical order, you can quickly find whatever topic you are looking for.

Third, *Can I do it and be a positive Christian witness?* This simple question will save a lot of headaches and heartaches later. You could also ask, *Would Jesus do this?* Testing the jokes you tell, music you listen to, movies you go see, TV shows you watch, books you read, and jobs you take through the "Jesus Filter" will answer a lot of your questions about the will of God!

Fourth, *Will the Lord be glorified?* In doing this, would I be honoring God with my body? Am I doing this so people will notice me, accept me, or think I'm cool? Am I seeking to please the Lord with this or I am hoping to become popular with a particular person or crowd?

There is a big difference between being *led* by the Spirit and being *driven* by the desire to please people. The first one is accompanied by a sense of peace and calmness, the second is filled with fear and anxiety.

Fifth, *Am I acting responsibly?* Are you being faithful to do the things you already know God wants you to do or are you bailing out because it is getting tough? God will not necessarily rescue us when we act irresponsibly. He will let us suffer the consequences in order to teach us to be faithful and dependable.

Proverbs 22:1 says that "A good name is more desirable than great riches; to be esteemed is better than silver or gold." Beware of "easy money" or "get rich quick" schemes that may require you to compromise your integrity. A damaged reputation is hard to repair.

Sixth, *Is it reasonable?* God expects us to think. While we shouldn't lean entirely on our own thoughts (Prov. 3:5-6), we are warned in the Bible not to shift our brains into neutral. God's guidance will likely go beyond what mere human reasoning could come up with, but His plan will not bypass your mind. First Corinthians 14:20 says, "Brethren, do not be children in your thinking; yet in evil be babes, but in your thinking be mature" (NASB).

False guidance from New Age teachers and deceiving spirits will often require the mind to be "turned off." Scripture, though, instructs us to think on things that are true, honorable, right, pure, of good reputation, excellent, and worthy of praise (Phil. 4:8).

Seventh, *Does a realistic opportunity exist?* Closed doors are not meant to be knocked down, but if the door is open and all other factors are in agreement, take the plunge. Remember, a closed door doesn't necessarily mean it will be closed forever; God may just want you to wait for His perfect timing.

Eighth, *Are parents and godly friends in agreement?*

Don't shy away from allowing your parents and others to ask you tough questions. Seek out their counsel; don't wait for them to come to you. If you don't have the answers to their objections, don't get upset. God may be using them to show you some blind spots in your thinking. Go back to God and His Word and think about what they have said to you.

If your parents say no, recognize that God is speaking through them. After all, if it isn't God's will, don't you want to know before you make the mistake of doing it? And remember, a "no" today doesn't necessarily mean a "no" forever. Don't make the mistake of rebelling against your parents. If you are certain that you are right, pray for your parents to have a change of heart. God is most likely using them to show you the right timing for His will.

Ninth, *Has God given me a strong desire to do this?* God often floods our hearts with joy when He is putting a plan or vision in our hearts. The joy of the Lord should be our strength (Neh. 8:10). But don't make the mistake of thinking that just because you feel excited about something, it must be God's will! It can be thrilling to think about trying to gratify a lust of the flesh. Make sure your joy comes from a Spirit-filled desire to see God's kingdom grow and people helped.

Tenth, *Do I have peace about it?* This is an inner peace. Is the peace of God guarding your heart and mind, or do you feel restless or uncomfortable when you think about this course of action? Warning bells should go off in your head if deep down inside there is a nagging feeling that what you are about to do is wrong, no matter how hard you try to rationalize it in your mind.

The true peace of God can be reigning in your heart, however, even if circumstances are against you. The Spirit of God alone can produce the kind of peace that goes beyond our understanding.

Have you been able to answer yes to all ten of these questions? If so, what are you waiting for? Go for it!

Are Your "Colors" Clear? _____

An African pastor was overrun by rebels who demanded that he renounce his faith in Jesus Christ. They swore they would kill him if he didn't. He didn't. Later, when the authorities discovered his body, they found the following words written on the wall of his house:

I am part of the "Fellowship of the Unashamed." I have Holy Spirit Power. The die has been cast. I've stepped over the line. The decision has been made. I am a disciple of His. I won't look back, let up, slow down, back away, or be still. My past is redeemed, my present makes sense, and my future is secure. I am finished and done with low living, sight-walking, small planning, smooth knees, colorless dreams, tame visions, mundane talking, chintzy giving, and dwarfed goals!

I no longer need preeminence, prosperity, position, promotions, plaudits, or popularity. I don't have to be right, first, tops, recognized, praised, regarded, or rewarded. I now live by presence, lean by faith, love by patience, lift by prayer, and labor by power.

My face is set, my gait is fast, my goal is heaven, my road is narrow, my way is rough, my companions few, my guide reliable, my mission clear. I cannot be bought, compromised, detoured, lured away, turned back, diluted, or delayed.

I will not flinch in the face of sacrifice, hesitate in the presence of adversity, negotiate at the table of the enemy, ponder at the pool of popularity, or meander in the maze of mediocrity. I won't give up, shut up, let up, or burn up till I've preached up, prayed up, paid up, stored up, and stayed up for the cause of Christ.

I am a disciple of Jesus. I must go till He comes, give till I drop, preach till all know, and work till He stops.

And when He comes to get His own, He'll have no problems recognizing me. My colors will be clear.[1]

Teenagers who are seeking the applause of the world are everywhere—hoping that they are beautiful enough, smart enough, rich enough, cool enough, successful enough, or strong enough to make it.

Teenagers who seek the applause of the One watching from "the heavenly grandstand" are few and far between. To God they are the most precious of diamonds—still rough and uncut perhaps, but rare and ready to burst forth in glory as the Master Jeweler chisels the imperfections away.

How about you? Are *your* "colors" clear? If you would like to tell God that you desire to find and follow His will alone, and that you want to live for His applause and not the world's, then would you join us as we pray?

Dear Lord, I thank You that I don't have to drift through life in confusion, never really sure that You guide my steps. I thank You for showing me how to walk in Your ways.

Father, keep me from looking for signs when You have already spoken so clearly through Your Word. Teach me to listen to my parents and to the wise counsel of godly people. I choose today to seek the wisdom that comes only from above, and I look forward to seeing how You will direct my steps as I walk in faith and dependence upon You.

I commit myself to seeking Your will, knowing Your will, and following Your will so You will be glorified. Thank You, Lord, for always walking with me, for I know that at times Your way will not be easy. Thank You that Your joy will be my strength and Your peace will guard my heart and mind all the way. Amen.

Wisdom Checklist _____

1. Have I prayed about it?   ☐ Yes   ☐ No

2. Is it consistent with the Word of God? ☐ Yes   ☐ No

3. Can I be a positive Christian witness? ☐ Yes   ☐ No

4. Will the Lord be glorified?   ☐ Yes   ☐ No

5. Am I acting responsibly?   ☐ Yes   ☐ No

6. Is it reasonable?   ☐ Yes   ☐ No
   What makes sense?
   What doesn't make sense?

7. Does a realistic opportunity exist?   ☐ Yes   ☐ No
   Factors for:
   Factors against:

8. Are parents and godly friends
   in agreement?   ☐ Yes   ☐ No
   Those for:
   Those against:

9. Has God given me a strong desire
   to do this?   ☐ Yes   ☐ No
   Why?
   Why not?

10. Do I have peace about it?   ☐ Yes   ☐ No
    Why?
    Why not?

PART 3

Walking
with
God

Believe It or Not!

After Sunday school class one morning, a mother asked her daughter what she had learned. The girl responded, "I learned how Moses built this awesome pontoon bridge across the Red Sea, and how all the Israelites were transported across it with tanks and armored personnel carriers. As soon as everyone was safely across, the bridge was blown up just as all the Egyptians were coming over it to get them. So the Egyptian army fell into the Red Sea and was drowned."

The mother was astonished and asked if that was what the teacher had really told the class.

"No," her daughter replied, "but you would never believe what she really said!"

That girl is like a lot of people. They think that faith is

somehow believing what couldn't possibly be true. Or they think that faith is just wishful thinking, without any solid basis for belief.

But that is not what Christian faith is like at all. True faith is putting your trust in what you *know* to be true, even though you don't see it with your eyes. It is reliance upon God's character and what He has promised. The key to knowing God's will is knowing His ways. The writer of Hebrews defined it for us when he wrote: "Now faith is being sure of what we hope for and certain of what we do not see" (Heb. 11:1).

Did you notice those key words—being *sure* and *certain*? Those words describe a condition of confidence and assurance, but not in what you can see with your eyes. Faith in God is seeing with spiritual eyes—eyes that have learned to see that God and His Word can be trusted!

Faith is how we get started in our Christian lives. Look at what Hebrews goes on to say: "And without faith it is impossible to please God, because anyone who comes to him must believe that he exists and that he rewards those who earnestly seek him" (Heb. 11:6).

Since God is not in the habit of showing up visibly and giving us a personal invitation to trust in Him, we have to come to Him by faith. Oh, He's there all right; we just can't see Him. But this should not be so hard for us since we are used to trusting in things we can't see—like air (unless you live in southern California!), microwaves, TV signals, sound waves, and ultraviolet radiation (for you sun gods and goddesses), just to name a few.

But our Christian lives don't just start with faith and stop. We are told in the Bible to "walk by faith, not by sight" (2 Cor. 5:7 NASB). Our whole lives are to be an ever-growing walk of faith in God.

We approach God in prayer with freedom and confidence *by faith* (Eph. 3:12). We stand against the fiery attacks of the devil by holding up the *shield of faith* (Eph. 6:16). We serve Christ *by faith* (1 Thess. 1:3). And so on. As Paul, the writer of Romans, says, "The righteous will live by faith" (Rom. 1:17).

Who Lives by Faith?

The funny thing is, though, that *everybody* lives by faith, whether they are Christians or not! For example, we all drive our cars by faith. You don't believe me? Well, imagine yourself behind the wheel for a minute. You are cruising down the road through a busy part of town. You see a green light up ahead. What do you do? You don't slow down or stop, you just keep going, right?

"How is that demonstrating faith?" you might ask. Simply this: If you are at a crossroads, you believe that drivers coming from the other direction will see their red light and stop. *You* never actually see the red light, do you? You are operating on faith—in this case, faith in the correct operation of the traffic lights, and faith in the safe driving habits of other drivers! In some cities that takes a *lot* of faith!

If you would stop and think about it, there are a million and one ways every day that both Christian and non-Christian people live by faith. We build friendships on faith and trust, and we do the same in dating relationships. We take tests in school by faith. We turn on the TV by faith. We even eat school cafeteria food by faith . . . lots of faith!

When I (Neil) was a little boy, I popped a coin into a vending machine and out came a bottle of soda pop. Without looking, I quickly took a swig of soda, but immediately spit it out. Then I noticed that the bottom of the bottle was filled with junk. I never drank that brand again!

Now we drink soft drinks out of *cans*! Talk about faith. And have you ever actually read the ingredients of what we are guzzling down? It's amazing how much faith we have in a brand name.

And that brings up an important point about faith. Once you lose trust in someone or something, it's hard to gain it back again, isn't it? Therefore, the real issue is not whether you are going to live by faith or not. We have already seen that you and I and everyone else on planet Earth lives by faith. What is the bottom line then? Simply this: Is the object of your faith trustworthy?

Who Ya Gonna Trust? _____

The Bible teaches that Jesus Christ is the author and perfecter of our faith (Heb. 12:2). Why is Jesus the ultimate object of faith? Because He is God. All He does is perfect and His Word is true. And every day of our lives we will find that He is reliable and trustworthy, because He never changes. Consider the following Scriptures:

> As for God, his way is perfect;
> > the word of the LORD is flawless.
> He is a shield
> > for all who take refuge in him. (Ps. 18:30)

> Remember your leaders, who spoke the word of God to you. Consider the outcome of their way of life and imitate their faith. Jesus Christ is the same yesterday and today and forever. (Heb. 13:7-8)

The sun is probably the most reliable object of faith for people in the world. It appears to be eternal and unchanging. It shows up every morning at a predictable time and drops out of sight in the same way each evening. We all just take for granted that it will do so tomorrow and the next day and the next.

Even when clouds block it from our sight or an eclipse hides it from view, we know the sun is still there. Without the sun, people couldn't survive. Our planet would soon become cold and uninhabitable. If the sun didn't rise tomorrow morning, what would happen to the world's faith? All of humanity would be thrown into total confusion!

If we have such great faith in the sun, why don't we have even greater faith in the Son who made the sun and the moon and the stars and the galaxies?

For all of us, from brand-new Christian to mature believer, our Christian lives are a process of shifting from trusting in ourselves to trusting in Jesus. As as we practice trusting Him, we learn from experience that He is faithful. As we relax in His faithfulness, we more easily discern His will.

Proverbs 28:25-26 makes it clear where our faith needs to be: "A greedy man stirs up dissension, but he who trusts in the LORD will prosper. / He who trusts in himself is a fool, but he who walks in wisdom is kept safe."

What do you believe will make you happy, satisfied, fulfilled, or successful in life? How you answer that question will show whether your faith is in God and His Word or in yourself and the world.

All of us grew up surrounded by a world system that does not believe what God says is true. And unless you were raised in a perfect Christian home, you bought into some of the garbage the world system offers. For example, if you believe that you will not be happy unless you have a girlfriend or boyfriend, you are setting yourself up for major disappointment. But if you believe that God loves you enough to provide what you need (including the right kind of relationships in *His* time), then you will be content and happy.

If you believe that success and happiness are defined by how much money you make or what possessions you have, you are again in for a rude awakening. Surely the richest (and wisest) man of his day, King Solomon, knew what he was talking about when he said: "Whoever loves money never has money enough; / whoever loves wealth is never satisfied with his income" (Eccl. 5:10).

Success, Joshua 1:8-9 tells us, comes from knowing the will of God for your life and doing it with confidence and boldness. True satisfaction will come to anyone who lives in the assurance that his life is pleasing to God.

If the world system hasn't distorted our faith enough as it is, the New Age movement has also thrown in its two cents—which is really *nonsense*. New Age teaching says that if you believe in something hard enough, it will become true. But believing something is true doesn't make it true. And *not* believing in something doesn't make it *not* true. Believing I deserve a BMW and visualizing it sitting in my driveway is not going to make it magically appear. And not believing in hell, for example, won't drop the temperature down there one degree!

You simply cannot and do not create reality with your mind. Only God can do that and we've got news for you, shocking as it may be: Jesus is God and you're not!

You Can't Make It Happen

To think that we will get what we want if we believe it with all our hearts is not faith in the promises of God's Word. It is simply faith based on our selfish desires and our energy. It starts in our own minds (not God's) and depends on our ability to believe (not on God's faithfulness to provide). It is a religious self-psych job and is nothing but worthless spiritual hype. It has nothing to do with the Christian faith.

Closely related are teachings that encourage people to "speak things into existence." These "positive confessors" will go around declaring themselves to be healthy while sneezing their brains out. Why? Because they believe "you possess what you confess."

The "Name it and claim it" (or "Blab it and grab it") gang are deceived as well. They are putting their faith in *their own words*, rather than in *God's Word*. God is simply under no obligation to do what we say. His only obligation is to be true to His character and to the promises He has written in the Bible.

True faith in God is shown by a quiet, humble dependence upon Him to provide what He says we need in His own perfect timing. No amount of our spiritual demands or temper tantrums will push God to act one second faster than He knows is best for us. And if you think about it, that should bring a deep sense of security. After all, who wants a God that can be pressured?

How much faith in God we have is determined by how well we know Him, as the psalmist made clear: "The LORD is a refuge for the oppressed, a stronghold in times of trouble. / Those who know your name will trust in you, for you, LORD, have never forsaken those who seek you" (Ps. 9:9-10).

Knowing God's name means knowing God personally and deeply. And the more you get to know God through His Word and the circumstances of life, the more you will "taste and see that the LORD is good" (Ps. 34:8). And your faith will grow deeper and stronger.

Rich's Dilemma

For many years I (Rich) felt a growing loneliness in my heart. As I look back, I see God was preparing me for marriage, but I was having so much fun in the ministry I rarely noticed my need . . . except when I was alone. During those times I would often cry out to God, wondering if I would ever find a wife. And seeing age thirty come and go with no prospects in sight only added to my fears.

The first question I had to wrestle with was this: Did God love me enough to meet my needs? I had grown to know Him well enough to say without hesitation, "Absolutely!" My faith had grown strong.

The second issue that I was struggling with was a little tougher: Will God take away my loneliness by providing a wife? That I didn't know for sure. I had to trust that my Father knew best. If it was His will for me to marry, He would have to move heaven and earth, because I was the classic "confirmed bachelor."

If God had decided that marriage was not best for me, I would have had to trust that He would remove my loneliness in another way. He would have met my needs through His wonderful presence and the body of Christ. Either way, I knew that God could be trusted.

Well, God provided Shirley Grace for me because He knew I *surely* needed a lot of *grace*! When I was thirty-three we began dating. A year and a half later we were engaged, and three months and one day after my thirty-fifth birthday, we were married. And six years later, we still are . . . praise God!

Question: If God wants it done, can it be done? Yes! That tried and true man of God, Job, said to the Lord: "I know that you can do all things; no plan of yours can be thwarted" (Job 42:2). If God wants me to do it, can I do it? Of course! "I can do all things through Him who strengthens me" (Phil. 4:13 NASB).

What are the "all things" those verses are talking about? Everything *we* want? No, everything *God* wants. "All things" means the things that are God's will—what He shows us in His Word. That's what we are to put our faith in. That's what we are to trust Him for. And we can be assured that God will always give us the power to do what He wants us to do.

But What If . . . ?

So how do we move on with life when God's will "ain't easy"? Is it possible to keep on keeping on with God when His will takes us on a detour we neither expected nor wanted? The life of a young man named Jeffrey will help answer that question. Let me introduce him to you.

When I (Rich) met him, he was a junior in high school, and he was crying. I was speaking on forgiving from the heart at the time, and something I said had deeply affected him.

After the message he came up and asked if we could talk. So we set up a time to meet the following morning—Jeffrey, his youth pastor, and I. There he told me his story.

Jeffrey had been born prematurely, and while being transported from one medical facility to another, he had been denied the precious oxygen his frail body needed. That neglect had resulted in severe physical damage.

He couldn't walk. His arms were barely usable and his hands were locked in kind of a clawlike position. His hip would give out frequently, and he had to get people to help him sit upright again in his wheelchair.

Although he had won a considerable amount of money in a lawsuit against the medical personnel, he had never been able to forgive them for what they had done to him. Understandably, Jeffrey was angry at God as well.

Jeffrey was a Christian and a strong one—don't get me wrong. And the quickness of his wit was surpassed only by the lightning speed of his intelligence. But he was hurting.

His sister had recently been healed supernaturally three months after suffering a crushing foot injury. Although

Jeffrey was happy for his sister, her healing only intensified the questions in his head. "Why her, Lord? Why not me?"

Some well-meaning believers had "prophesied" that Jeffrey would walk again. A doctor had even given him the impression that a back operation would enable him to finally leave his wheelchair behind. It never happened.

As he was relating all of this to me, I prayed for wisdom. "Jeffrey," I said slowly, "I don't want to say anything that is going to sound like a cliché."

He nodded, knowing exactly what I meant.

"But your happiness as a person simply cannot be dependent upon your physical condition." I hoped that my heart, which was breaking for this young man, was coming through my words.

"I know that," Jeffrey replied sincerely.

"Jeffrey, there are thousands and thousands of Christians out there who are able-bodied and can walk. But they are in emotional and spiritual bondage. You, however, have the opportunity to wheel out of this room today a free man!"

What happened after that was incredible. As we prayed together, he began to forgive the doctors who had hurt him. He let go of his anger toward God. By faith he thanked God for every part of his body that didn't work right. Then he committed himself once again to the Lord's care and gave each part of his body to God to be used for His glory.

After it was all over, Jeffrey's face was radiant through his tears. And so was mine.

Does he still use a wheelchair? Yes. But Jeffrey walks by faith in the God who *will* one day in heaven say, "Rise up and walk!" And then he will be completely healed forever. For now, though, a healed soul is enough.

Do you see? It *is* possible to walk by faith when things are tough! Just ask Jeffrey.

It should be clear by now that faith is more than just agreeing in your head that something is true. It is not passive; it is active. True biblical faith results in action. For Jeffrey, it was choosing to forgive and release his anger. It was thanking God for his body and committing it to the Lord for His use. And it meant moving on with his life, trusting in Jesus to make it all that He wants it to be.

Faith Is More Than an Attitude _____

You may have heard the story of the circus performer who strung a wire over Niagara Falls and rode across it on a unicycle. The crowd that had gathered to watch him was in awe. When he returned, everyone went crazy, cheering and applauding his incredible feat.

Then he asked, "Who believes I can do that again with a man on my shoulders?" The crowd roared in approval. They believed he could do it! "All right, then," he continued, "who will hop on?" No one said a word.

You see, the person who hops on the performer's shoulders is the one who truly believes. Faith is not just thought, it's action, as James preached so clearly:

What good is it, my brothers, if a man claims to have faith but has no deeds? Can such faith save him? Suppose a brother or sister is without clothes and daily food. If one of you says to him, "Go, I wish you well; keep warm and well fed," but does nothing about his physical needs, what good is it? In the same way, faith by itself, if it is not accompanied by action, is dead. (James 2:14-17)

No, good works do not save you. We are saved by the grace of God through faith (Eph. 2:8-9). But true saving faith will *result* in good works (Eph. 2:10). Let your true faith in Christ radiate to those around you by fervent prayers, kind words of love and wisdom, and helpful deeds that meet people's needs.

"Faith" that has no works is a false faith, a demonic counterfeit of the real thing. Even the devil knows who Christ is and what He accomplished in His death and resurrection. Even though the demons know the Bible backward and forward, they are not saved. In fact, they shudder when they think of God (James 2:19). They are committed to trying to stop everything that God is doing in the world.

Satan's plan is to discredit God and erode our confidence in His Word. But if there is a counterfeit, then there must be the real thing. If there are deceiving spirits, there must be a Holy Spirit who will guide us into all truth. Notice how we are to respond to what is false and choose what is true:

> *Beloved, do not believe every spirit, but test the spirits to see whether they are from God; because many false prophets have gone out into the world. . . . You are from God, little children, and have overcome them; because greater is He who is in you than he who is in the world. . . . For whatever is born of God overcomes the world; and this is the victory that has overcome the world—our faith. And who is the one who overcomes the world, but he who believes that Jesus is the Son of God? (1 John 4:1, 4; 5:4-5* NASB)

"Ain't nothin' like the real thing, baby!" That slogan refers to a lot more than soft drinks. It applies to life as well. The "real thing" is going to meet our deepest needs, whether in life or in death. The real thing is Jesus Christ. No other will cut it when life itself is on the line.

We'll close this chapter with one more story of faith.

At the end of July 1976, a group of leadership women from Campus Crusade for Christ were enjoying a retreat at a ranch at the base of the Big Thompson River canyon. That steep canyon drops off from the town of Estes Park, Colorado, to flatter land down near the town of Loveland.

One evening a tremendous thunderstorm exploded over

Estes Park and dumped about eight inches of rain on that rocky terrain. The land, not having the soil to absorb that amount of water, simply funneled the rain into the river.

Because of the severity of the storm, power lines were down and phones were out down at the ranch site. Unknown to the women who were there, a flash flood warning had been issued and evacuation of the canyon was under way.

Fortunately, two police cars came down the canyon, sirens blaring and loudspeakers warning of the emergency. The women piled into a couple of vehicles and followed the police cars away from the ranch.

Unfortunately, one of the police cars went the wrong way and led a car jammed with eight women back up into the canyon. They drove right into the teeth of the flood.

Those who witnessed the water crashing down the Big Thompson River said it was a twenty-foot-high wall of water. The flood's momentum swept entire trees, boulders, and parts of homes downstream with it.

As the water steadily filled up the car with the eight women inside, one of them miraculously squeezed out through a window and swam to safety. She later told the story of what had happened in that vehicle.

She said that as the reality of drowning hit them, all eight were singing to the Lord, "Thank You, Jesus. Thank You, Jesus."

The next day a temporary morgue was set up in a large community room. Hundreds had perished in the flood. It was the job of some of the Campus Crusade staff to see if the bodies of the seven women had been recovered. If so, they had to identify them.

When they mentioned to the man who was overseeing the bodies that they were looking for seven Christian women from Campus Crusade, his face immediately showed recognition.

"Come this way, please. I think I know which ones they are," he said.

They wound their way through the sheet-covered corpses until the man stopped. He pulled off seven sheets, revealing the leadership women.

"How did you know these were the ones we were looking for?" the men asked, puzzled.

"When you told me they were Christians, I knew. It's their faces. Their faces are like the faces of angels. All the others have faces twisted and contorted in agony and terror. That's how I knew."

Is this merely a tragic account of seven young women who died before their time? Not really. You see, the parents of the ladies gave permission for their stories to be printed in the newspaper—actually in hundreds of newspapers all across the country. Millions of people read about their faith, and only God knows how many were touched by the saving power of the Lord Jesus Christ as a result of the women's lives and deaths.

Was it worth it to those seven women who lived and died trusting in the One who had died and risen for them? Well, they're in heaven now, so I guess we can't ask them. But somehow I think we already know what they'd say.

We have the privilege to walk by faith in the God who has shown Himself through all of time to be trustworthy. Hebrews 11 contains a partial list of God's Faith Hall of Fame—men and women throughout the Bible who have walked by faith and found God to be faithful. We happen to think that God is still adding names to that list of faithful followers. We think there were probably seven more names added in July 1976. And we'd like our names one day to be entered into the Faith Hall of Fame.

How about you? Would you join with us in expressing our thanks to God for His faithful presence and power?

Dear heavenly Father, You are the One I trust. You are ultimately the only reliable and completely faithful One. It is You I believe in. You are the way and the truth and the life. You hold all things together by Your powerful Word.

Forgive me for the many times I became anxious or fearful and did not walk by faith in You. Forgive me for the times I assumed I knew what Your will was without bothering to ask You. I figured You would just bless all my plans. I was wrong for doing that. Thank You for Your forgiveness.

I want to know Your ways so that I can know Your will and grow in my faith. I ask You to fill me with the Holy Spirit and guide me into the way of truth. I ask that You would not lead me into temptation, but deliver me from the evil one.

I pray that You would never allow me to lead another person astray by my words or my example, but allow others to be strengthened in their walk of faith through Your gracious working in my life. To You be all glory. Amen.

CHAPTER 12

Becoming a Spiritual Detective

I (Rich) had just finished speaking at a youth conference when a teenage girl and her youth leader came up to me. They were excited about what God had done in their lives, but the girl was still a little bit confused by something.

Her youth leader explained that for months they had been trying to get rid of Mario. No, Mario was not an ex-boyfriend or anything like that. Mario, it turned out, had been a "friend" of a different kind. He was an invisible friend, sometimes called an "imaginary friend." But there was nothing "imaginary" about him.

Mario had been with Kelsey (not her real name) for a long time. He never seemed to give her any really bad advice. As a matter of fact, much of what he told her was quite helpful. The main problem with Mario was that Kelsey had come to lean on him far more than God.

Just before I met her, Kelsey had gone through *The Steps to Freedom in Christ* with the rest of the group. After finishing up, she tried to reach Mario.

"Mario! Mario!" she called, but no voice responded in her head. "Mario, are you there?" She tried again, but with the same result.

The youth leader went on to tell me that a few weeks prior to the conference, they had tried to take Kelsey through *The Steps to Freedom in Christ* by herself. But Mario had kept her up all night, so she was too exhausted the next day to go through them.

"What do you think Mario was?" I asked Kelsey.

"I don't know," she replied, shaking her head in confusion.

"Mario was a spirit guide, a demon pretending to be your friend," I explained.

In reality, Mario had not been her friend but her enemy. I told Kelsey to renounce (verbally reject) conversing with Mario, and she told him to go away and never come back.

"And if Mario ever tries to come back, don't invite him in!" I warned her. "Even if *Super* Mario shows up, tell him to beat it in Jesus' name!"

Kelsey, like so many others—both Christian and non-Christian, had been deceived. Satan's favorite tactic is *deception,* misleading us so that we fall for one of his traps. What is our weapon of defense against deception? It is *discernment*—the ability to distinguish between truth and lies, and between good and evil.

Discernment is a critical part of our walk with God. It is a supernatural ability given to us by the Holy Spirit. It is our first line of defense when our own knowledge or experience is not enough to protect us. It is God's warning bell that goes off within our spirit, telling us that something is wrong.

One day I (Rich) was riding a bus in Birmingham, England. My back was toward the front of the bus since I was talking to some high school kids behind me. All of a sudden I had this awful sense of the presence of evil. The impression was so strong, I whirled around to the front just as two Mormon missionaries got on the bus.

Was there any "rational" way for me to know that two members of a cult were climbing on that bus at that very moment? No. Could it have been lucky coincidence? I don't think so. Then what was happening?

Clearly, the Holy Spirit within me was bearing witness that an unholy spirit (demon) was approaching. That was my first line of defense. Immediately I was on my spiritual toes. Once I saw the cult members, my mind recognized the reason for the spiritual siren that God had set off inside of me. Then I could pray and ask the Lord to protect the young Christian students who were with me.

Our Fearless Leader

Jesus Christ had 100 percent perfect discernment into the hearts of men and the presence of evil. We don't. But we have been given the Holy Spirit, and He can train us to be the "spiritual detectives" we need to be in a world filled with deception.

The Holy Spirit who lives within all believers in Christ is the Spirit of *truth*, as He said in John 16:13-15 and reaffirmed in 1 John 2:20-21:

> *For the Holy Spirit has come upon you, and you know the truth. So I am not writing to you as to those who need to know the truth, but I warn you as those who can discern the difference between true and false. (1 John 2:20-21 TLB)*

John is *not* saying that studying the Bible is no longer

necessary. What he is saying, however, is that the Holy Spirit inside us will be our guide as we go through life. He will teach us to discern truth and lies. He will disclose to us what the Word of Christ really means and how we should obey it. He will warn us of spiritual danger.

Truth is what keeps us from the evil one; truth is God's will made known through His Word (John 17:15, 17). The key, then, to developing a discerning heart is to let the Spirit of truth (the Holy Spirit) guide you into understanding the truth (the Bible), as spoken by the Truth (Jesus Christ)!

Chose Your Label: Spiritual or Carnal?

Many Christians do not have their "spiritual antennae" up, nor are their "spiritual radios" tuned to God's station. We call these kinds of Christians "carnal," "worldly," or "fleshly." To live in a carnal manner is tragic, because deception is all around us. It is so easy to let our guards down and be duped by some false teaching, even by a demonic impression directly placed into our minds.

Carnal Christians choose to walk according to their flesh. The apostle Paul wrote to them this way:

Brothers, I could not address you as spiritual but as worldly—mere infants in Christ. I gave you milk, not solid food, for you were not yet ready for it. Indeed, you are still not ready. You are still worldly. For since there is jealousy and quarreling among you, are you not wordly? Are you not acting like mere men? (1 Cor. 3:1-3)

Carnal Christians tend to neglect the Word of God and live instead according to the false beliefs of sinful society. These spiritually defeated Christians fail to put on the armor of God and end up paying attention to deceiving spirits. They foolishly ignore the presence of the Holy Spirit within them, and therefore place themselves in grave spiritual danger.

On the other hand, there is Spiritual Man. He sounds like a super-hero, doesn't he? . . . complete with a big "S" on his chest! Well, I guess you could call him a super*natural* hero—a hero of the faith.

Spiritual Man is learning to think and act according to the truth (Eph. 4:21, 23). He has the mind of Christ and is using it to discern the truth (1 Cor. 2:15–16). He studies the Word of truth (the Bible) so that he can know the truth and use it correctly (2 Tim. 2:15). He walks in freedom from the bondage of sin and Satan, because the truth sets him free (John 8:32). He lives his life in the power of the Holy Spirit, not in the energy of the flesh, and so the fruit of the Spirit is evident in his life (Gal. 5:16-23).

A good example of a Spiritual Man was King Solomon in the early days of his reign. When God told Solomon he could have whatever he wanted, the king asked for a wise and discerning heart. Solomon could have selfishly asked for great riches, a long life, or easy military victory, but he didn't. And so God gave him more wisdom than any other man who ever lived—apart from Christ, of course (1 Kings 3:8-12).

God gave Solomon a wise and discerning heart because his motives were pure. Solomon humbly recognized his need to know right from wrong and good from evil, asked God to help him, and God did.

True discernment from God is given to those whose motive is love. Wrong motives open the door for Satan's counterfeits.

A few years ago, a college girl was following me (Neil) around to my different speaking engagements. After one evening service, she was shaking visibly. I saw her struggle and asked if I could help. She agreed to stop by my office the next day.

The girl admitted she had problems and said she was seeing a Christian counselor, but she wasn't taking the sessions seriously. It seems she could tell everything the counselor was going to do next, so she enjoyed playing mind games with him. When I saw the destructive path she was on, I challenged her.

"You like doing that, don't you? You like the advantage it gives you over other people."

The girl believed that God had given her a gift of mind reading that enabled her to point out people's sins. But when I helped her find freedom in Christ, that ability disappeared. It wasn't the Holy Spirit giving her discernment. It was an evil spirit pretending to be the Spirit of God.

How had the demon gained access to her life? Most likely through her pride. The girl's motives had not been pure—she proudly gloated over her ability to know other people's secrets instead of weeping over their sins and restoring them in love.

The Bible talks about the "distinguishing of spirits" (1 Cor. 12:10 NASB), which refers to a spiritual gift. The Holy Spirit can enable us to distinguish between a good spirit and an evil one. Some people have a special spiritual gift to do this, but all of us have the responsibility to be on the watch for counterfeits.

While spiritual discernment is mainly a function of the Spirit, not the mind, it does require our brains. And the spiritual gift of discernment doesn't replace the need to know the truth from God's Word, but builds upon the truth that we already understand. Many times the Holy Spirit will alert us that something is wrong. That is discernment. Then our minds automatically begin searching for *what* is wrong. That may not come right away, and we need to pray that God will reveal what the problem is in His time.

Let me (Neil) illustrate. Suppose my son comes home and I sense that something is wrong. So I ask him, "What's wrong, Karl?"

He says, "Nothin'!"

Again I ask him what's wrong, and again he claims that "nothin'" is wrong. My "buzzer" is going off because I am discerning that something *is* wrong.

This is the point at which we usually blow it. We think we're pretty smart so we try and guess what the problem is. We might start asking questions like, "Karl, have you been doing such and such again?" If I guess wrong (and I probably will), I blow the opportunity discernment gave me. Karl will stalk away into his room, mad at me for falsely accusing him.

So what should I do? Just share the discernment: "Karl, something is wrong."

"No, Dad, nothin's wrong!"

"Karl, I *know* something is wrong."

He'll shrug his shoulders and go to his room. But is that the end of it? No, not at all! Remember, the Holy Spirit made me aware that something was wrong, and after I expressed that, God had a direct shot at Karl in his bedroom.

Guess what will happen in his room? Conviction! I can imagine what he'll be thinking—*Dad knows!* And he will consent to share the problem with me.

Sometimes the Holy Spirit gives us more than just a warning that evil is present. Sometimes He gives us distinct impressions of what the problem is. This kind of leading from the Lord occurs quite often in our counseling sessions.

For example, I (Rich) and a mature Christian woman were counseling a troubled young lady. All of a sudden I sensed the Lord directing me to gently ask her if she had ever had an abortion. She had actually endured two of them. Confessing her involvement and experiencing her Father's forgiveness turned out to be important pieces of the puzzle in finding her freedom in Christ.

We must ask the Lord to guide us in sharing these thoughts. We must speak the truth in love (Eph. 4:15), remembering that a gentle answer turns away wrath (Prov. 15:1).

But none of us is perfect. Sometimes our impressions are simply not something the counselee struggles with. Sometimes the impressions are accurate, but the person is not ready to face the truth. That's why a kind spirit and a patient attitude are essential.

It's important to note that even if our impressions *are* true, they are not "scriptural revelations," and they are definitely no substitute for knowing the Bible.

Our ability to discern grows in proportion to our spiritual maturity and our knowledge of God and His ways. There are no shortcuts to maturity. We must first drink milk before we eat meat. That is, we must first learn the basics of the faith before moving on to deeper spiritual truths. We must first mature in love before we can discern what is best for ourselves and others with a pure heart (Phil. 1:9-10).

Discernment without love leads to a critical, judgmental spirit of self-righteous superiority. Jesus sternly warned against that kind of attitude when He said:

Do not judge, or you too will be judged. For in the same way you judge others, you will be judged, and with the measure you use, it will be measured to you. Why do you look at the speck of sawdust in your brother's eye and pay no attention to the plank in your own eye? How can you say to your brother, "Let me take the speck out of your eye," when all the time there is a plank in your own eye? You hypocrite, first take the plank out of your own eye, and then you will see clearly to remove the speck from your brother's eye. (Matt. 7:1-5)

Discernment *with* love produces love, hope, and freedom in Christ.

The Angel Craze

One major area of deception in America today concerns the latest spiritual "fad"—angels. If ever there was an instance in which discernment is needed, it's this one! Unfortunately, lots of people are being spiritually duped by this angel craze. You might call it "Gullible's Travels."

Nearly 2,000 years ago, the apostle Paul warned us that evil spirits would impersonate God's angels when he wrote: "Satan himself masquerades as an angel of light" (2 Cor. 11:14).

An angel of light! This is the big league of wicked deception. Don't assume that any supernatural being surrounded by light that appears to someone must be from God. Remember, demons are master impersonators. They will even go so far as to talk about God, love, joy, prayer, our need to love others, and so on. Just like a counterfeit twenty-dollar bill, they can look so much like the real thing that it is hard to distinguish them.

A recent TV show featured stories of how angels helped people. It was kind of a *Rescue 911* of the spiritual world. One man named Andy overdosed on cocaine. He managed to crawl back to his apartment and get in the shower. While in the shower, some angels whirled around him and apparently saved his life.

Several days later three angels surrounded by light appeared to him and zapped him in the forehead with a talent for painting. (The forehead, by the way, just happens to be the location of the "third" or psychic eye in the occult.) The angels then commanded him to paint two thousand angel pictures by the year 2000. He has already completed hundreds of them. Supposedly even the pope has one of his paintings.

I (Rich) saw some examples of his artwork. Whatever he got zapped with wasn't God-given talent! His angels look more like fish! And indeed there is something very "fishy" about the whole thing.

Aside from the quality of the paintings, what's wrong with two thousand angel pictures? A lot. True angels from God don't point people to angels; they point people to the true God—the Lord Jesus Christ.

Twice in the book of Revelation, the apostle John fell at the feet of an angel to worship him. Both times the angel quickly stopped him. In Revelation 19:10, John recorded the angel's words in one of those instances: "Do not do it! I am a fellow servant with you and with your brothers who hold to the testimony of Jesus. Worship God!"

Beware of stories of so-called "guardian angels" developing long-term friendships with people. That simply never happens in the Bible. Be on the alert as well when the angels tell people their names. In Scripture, angels appeared as messengers to many people, such as Abraham, Balaam, Gideon, Daniel, Joseph, Mary, and others. Not once did any of them identify itself as a "guardian angel." Only once (in the case of Gabriel) did the angelic messenger give his name. And in only one case did the angel appear to someone several times over a period of time. That was when Joseph had to be warned by an angel repeatedly in dreams to move the young Jesus to safety. There is, however, never any indication in the Bible of angels and men developing anything close to a friendship.

What is rare or nonexistent in the Bible has become commonplace in our easily deceived nation. We must learn to judge what we experience by what the Bible says . . . not the other way around!

So what is the truth? Do God's angels actually come to

earth and help people? Let's let the Bible do the talking: "Are not all angels ministering spirits sent to serve those who will inherit salvation?" (Heb. 1:14).

Indeed, God sends His messengers to help His people. The Bible is very clear on that. We cannot, however, call them and make them come to us. God sends them when He knows it's best.

Sometimes those who encounter angels do not recognize them to be angels, as the writer of Hebrews goes on to tell us: "Do not forget to entertain strangers, for by so doing some people have entertained angels without knowing it" (Heb. 13:2).

God's angels can take on human form. They did so when they rescued Lot from the destruction of the city of Sodom (Gen. 19). Many times, however, the majestic presence of an angel created such terror in the person that the angel had to tell him, "Do not be afraid" (e.g., Luke 1:12-13).

Certainly a demonic spirit can instill fear as well. Are there any other ways to check out an alleged angel to see if it is really legit? You can carefully examine the message it brings. Does it teach anything contrary to the truth of God's Word?

On that same TV show we mentioned before, a man named Vern said he received messages from angels who spoke directly into his mind. They would point him to people who needed help, some of whom were suicidal, and he was able to prevent a number of people from taking their lives.

As I watched I said, "Lord, this seems really good. Is it from You?" (That, by the way, is always a really smart question to ask God any time you are confused or in doubt.)

The story went on to describe a message Vern received in the middle of the night. It startled him out of his sleep. "Find the boy with the rose," the voice told him. For days he carefully searched the sidewalks as he drove his car, looking for a boy carrying a rose. No luck.

One day he felt compelled to go into a coffee shop he'd not been in for a while. There he tried to talk with a troubled and somewhat hostile young man. As the boy reached for something, his sleeve pulled back to reveal the tattoo of a rose on his arm! This young man was going to take his own life, but Vern was able to talk him out of it.

I was still confused by whether Vern's power was from God or not. Then the truth came out. Vern died and "the boy with the rose" showed up at the funeral to tell Vern's widow the story of how he had helped him. According to the woman's own words, Vern had told the young man his views about *reincarnation*. That is what had convinced him not to commit suicide.

Bingo! Vern was not being directed by an angel from God. He was dealing with a demon, a spirit guide posing as an angel. How do I know that? Because the Bible does not teach reincarnation; it teaches *resurrection*. And though some of Vern's actions produced temporary good—the saving of lives—his source of power was evil (Matt. 7:15-17).

John writes, "Beloved, do not believe every spirit, but test the spirits to see whether they are from God; because many false prophets have gone out into the world" (1 John 4:1 NASB). This is a command, not an option. We are required by God to test the spirits. The Spirit of God will enable us to do so as we follow His leading and as we diligently study the Word of God.

Let's not waste this precious resource that God has made available to us—the ability by the Holy Spirit to discern good and evil, right and wrong, and truth and lies. The times are too spiritually dangerous to be lazy. We need to be on the cutting edge of our faith. God has put us on "Red Alert." Will you join us as we pray?

Dear heavenly Father, I desire to know You and Your ways. I don't want to take any shortcuts and be deceived by evil spirits. I want to know the truth, and Jesus is the truth. Give me the strength I need to diligently study Your Word so that my mind is made new.

I want others to see Your love in me. May that be the proof that I am Your disciple. Please protect me from thinking that I am a spiritual "know-it-all." I confess my pride to You. I humble myself before You and ask You to fill me with the Holy Spirit.

I ask You to lead me into all truth, so that I can discern good and evil. Give me the courage to expose the lies and deception around me, but let me always do it with a heart filled with love. I ask all this in Jesus' name, amen.

Walking Hand in Hand with God

A young pilot was flying solo when suddenly the weather turned bad. He didn't have enough gas to turn back, so he had no choice but to push on. Visibility dropped to near zero as the fog rolled in. He couldn't see where he was going, so he had to rely completely on his cockpit instruments. He had been trained to do so, but now it was life or death. To say he was nervous would be an understatement!

The idea of landing was the scariest. He had to fly into a crowded, big-city airport, and he'd never been there before. In a few minutes he would be in radio contact with the tower, but for now he was alone with his thoughts.

It would have been so easy to panic. Twice he reached for the radio to broadcast a Mayday, but he forced himself to go over and over the words of his instructor instead. His instructor had practically forced him to memorize the rule book. He had hated it at the time, but now he was glad he did it.

Finally he heard the voice of the air traffic controller. Trying not to sound too nervous, the young pilot asked for landing instructions.

"I'm going to put you on a holding pattern," the controller responded.

Great! thought the pilot. But deep down he knew that his safe landing was in the hands of the man in the tower. After all, the controller had radar and knew much better than he did what was going on around him.

The pilot had to draw upon all his previous instruction and training and trust in an air traffic controller he could not see. The words of the old hymn, "Trust and obey, for there's no other way," came alive to him. Aware that this was not the place to be cocky, he told the controller, "This is not a seasoned pro up here. I would appreciate any help you could give me."

"You got it!" he heard back.

For the next forty-five minutes, the controller gently guided the young pilot through the blinding fog. Every once in a while he would instruct him to alter his course or altitude. The pilot realized that the controller was guiding him around obstacles and away from possible collisions.

With the words of the rule book clearly in mind and the soothing voice of the controller in his headset, the pilot landed safely at last.

Just like the air traffic controller, the Holy Spirit guides us through the confusing and sometimes dangerous fogs of life. The controller assumed that the young pilot understood the instructions of the flight manual. His guidance was based on that. In the same way, the Holy Spirit asks us to rely on the Word of God and uses it to guide us.

The flight instruction manual taught the truth about how the pilot should fly. But did the manual give the pilot the *power* to fly? Of course not. The plane had an engine, and that was the source of its power. In addition, the air traffic controller was needed to help the pilot fly *safely*. He instructed the pilot on things the pilot couldn't see: his location, other aircraft, how and when to land.

It is not enough for you as a Christian to know your instruction manual, the Bible. You must rely on your air traffic controller, the Holy Spirit, to guide you around unseen obstacles and over an unknown path. The Spirit of God also gives us understanding of what the Bible is saying.

Do you see that a balance is necessary? Both the Word and the Spirit, the Spirit and the Word.

Tug-of-War

So what does it mean to walk in the Spirit? How do we know if that is happening in our lives? Let's begin by looking closely at Paul's teaching in Galatians 5:16-18:

> But I say, walk by the Spirit, and you will not carry out the desire of the flesh. For the flesh sets its desire against the Spirit, and the Spirit against the flesh, for these are in opposition to one another, so that you may not do the things that you please. But if you are led by the Spirit, you are not under the law. (NASB)

Have you ever felt like there was a tug-of-war going on inside you and that your mind was the rope? That is the conflict that occurs inside every believer in Christ. It is the constant battle between our flesh and the Spirit.

Our flesh is the part of us that grows up learning how to live life apart from Christ. We learn to relate to people in selfish ways. We figure out ways to protect ourselves from pain and defend ourselves against rejection, failure, and discouragement. We know these ways are not God's ways, but unfortunately, all these sinful habits are not magically wiped out when we trust Christ as Savior.

God's Spirit comes to live inside of us, however, the moment we trust Jesus Christ as Savior and Lord. He is constantly trying to direct us and empower us to live according to God's ways. The Spirit's working is in direct opposition to the flesh. He urges us to follow God's ways instead of just doing what we please.

So this is the first question we need to ask: Are we pleasing ourselves or are we seeking to please God? Galatians 5:13 puts it this way: "You were called to freedom, brethren; only do not turn your freedom into an opportunity for the flesh, but through love serve one another" (NASB).

If we are just doing what we want, without regard for God's teachings, we are not walking in the Spirit; we are walking according to the flesh. But if we are loving and serving others, obeying the Word, we are walking according to the Spirit. "The fruit of the Spirit is love" (Gal. 5:22-23).

Licentious or Legalistic?

When I (Rich) was young, I had a dog named Sam. Sam had a dog license on his collar and that was appropriate, because he was the classic *licentious* dog. Licentious means he did what he wanted and didn't listen to anybody. For Sam, rules were made to be broken and he broke all of them!

Whenever he got the chance, Sam would escape from the house. If we left the door open one second too long, he would be gone. While outside he would stand in the street and bark at cars. He chased bicyclists and joggers, trying to bite their feet. He was not vicious; he was just a pain in the neck (or the foot!).

One day Sam escaped and was gone for several hours.

Suddenly we saw him racing up the street toward our house. We had placed a pan of water outside near the door, hoping to lure him close enough to grab him. We didn't need it. We simply threw open the door and he bolted right in at full speed.

And then we smelled it. Sam had been skunked! Chaos broke out. My dad, mom, brother, and I went crazy trying to catch our poor tortured dog before he stunk up everything in the house. Finally, my mom grabbed him, dragged him out into the garage, and washed him down with tomato juice. What an absolutely humiliating experience for such a macho dog!

Sam is like a lot of Christians. They refuse to follow their Master's orders. They ignore His Word. They view His commands as "cramping their style" rather than protecting them from harm. They presume on God's mercy, figuring that He will simply get them out of whatever mess they get into. God never promises to do that. There are no guarantees against getting seriously "skunked" in life, if you choose to live according to the flesh. In fact, there can be very painful consequences to sin—even for believers—as Galatians 6:7-8 points out:

> Do not be deceived, God is not mocked; for whatever a man sows, this he will also reap. For the one who sows to his own flesh shall from the flesh reap corruption, but the one who sows to the Spirit shall from the Spirit reap eternal life. (NASB)

If we choose to walk by the flesh, we are responsible for the consequences of the choices we make. If we walk by the Spirit, God says He assumes responsibility for the consequences.

Is there a way out for the licentious Christian? Of course there is. But it's not tomato juice. It's another red fluid, far more precious. It is the blood of Jesus, available for cleansing to all who own up to their sin before God:

> *If we say that we have fellowship with Him and yet walk in the darkness, we lie and do not practice the truth; but if we walk in the light as He Himself is in the light, we have fellowship with one another, and the blood of Jesus His Son cleanses us from all sin. (1 John 1:6-7 NASB)*

Many Christians, however, fall into the error that is the opposite of licentiousness. This is called *legalism*—living by certain rules and regulations in the hope that doing so will earn God's favor and produce a spiritual life. This is living life "under the law" and is not God's plan for living. It has nothing to do with walking by the Spirit. Galatians 5:18 makes that crystal clear when it says: "If you are led by the Spirit, you are not under the Law" (NASB).

The legalistic person tends to live under a lot of guilt, especially as he becomes painfully aware of how often he fails. To cope with that guilt, he may stick his nose into the lives of others. When he observes their failure, he can become critical and judgmental of them. A harsh, prideful spirit can develop as he begins to consider himself better or more spiritual than others.

Legalistic churches keep people under control by guilt. To the poor people in those congregations, the gospel isn't good news, it's bad news. There is little joy in life as God seems stern and difficult to please. It is no wonder that many teenagers brought up in such a strict, stifling church environment chuck their religion as soon as they can! To them, freedom seems far more likely to be found in a bar than in Christ.

In addition to what we've already mentioned, there are three main reasons why trying to live according to the law doesn't work.

First, the law (which shows us our sin) was meant to lead us to Christ, and Christ is the end of the law to all who believe (Gal. 3:24; Rom. 10:4).

Once we come to Christ, we are accepted completely by Him (Rom. 15:7). There is therefore no longer any need to keep up some impossible standard of spiritual performance in order to earn God's favor. We already have it, because we are children of God! Listen to the refreshing words of John: "How great is the love the Father has lavished upon us, that we should be called children of God! And that is what we are!" (1 John 3:1).

God loves us because in Christ we are His kids. He loves us when we are bad and He loves us when we are good. And that love and kindness are like a magnet that draws us back to God in repentance from our sin (Rom. 2:4).

Once we become spiritually alive in Christ, we have the power within us to walk by the Spirit and not carry out the desires of the flesh. The Christian life isn't about trying to stop sinning by our own efforts, it is about walking by faith in God's truth in the power of the Holy Spirit.

Second, the law is powerless to give life. Telling people that what they are doing is wrong does not give them the ability to stop. God's Spirit is the energizer in our spirits that gives us the desire and power to obey God, as Paul explained in Philippians 2:12-13:

Therefore, my dear friends, as you have always obeyed—not only in my presence, but now much more in my absence— continue to work out your salvation with fear and trembling, for it is God who works in you to will and to act according to his good purpose.

Finally, the law can actually stimulate the desire to do wrong! Try telling a child he can't go into a certain room of the house, and immediately where does he want to go?

When I (Neil) was young, I had some friends who were Catholic. Their church posted a list of movies that the teenagers were not allowed to watch. That quickly became the list of the hottest movies to go see! My friends actually tore the list off the wall of the church and shared it with the entire high school campus.

The problem is not with God's laws. They are good and holy. The problem is that our flesh is so inclined to do wrong that all it needs is a little direction and it is off and running. Romans 7:8 hits the nail on the head: "But sin used this law against evil desires by reminding me that such desires are wrong and arousing all kinds of forbidden desires within me!" (TLB).

We're not trying to tell you that God's moral standards are not needed! Of course we need moral standards. How else would we know right from wrong? But the way we relate to God is by faith, and only the presence of the Holy Spirit inside us can give us the power to do the will of God.

So if walking by the Spirit is not license and it's not legalism, what is it? It is liberty: "Now the Lord is the Spirit; and where the Spirit of the Lord is, there is liberty" (2 Cor. 3:17 NASB).

Walking by the Spirit means that we do not sit around expecting God to do everything for us. We need to step out in faith, believing that He will give us power *as we go*. But *walking* by the Spirit also means that we are not running around in endless activity trying to make the Christian life happen by our own efforts.

Think about this: How much work would get done for God's kingdom if we expected God to do everything? Nothing! How much work would get done if we tried to do it all by ourselves? Nothing! We have the privilege to plant the seeds and water them, but it is God who causes the growth (1 Cor. 3:7-8).

The Yoke's on You _____

Perhaps no other verses in the Bible are more relevant to today's hurried and worried world than Jesus' invitation in Matthew 11:28-30. If the Christian life seems like a burden to you, if you are worn out, wiped out, burned out, or stressed out, then listen to Jesus and breathe a sigh of relief:

> *Come to me, all you who are weary and burdened, and I will give you rest. Take my yoke upon you and learn from me, for I am gentle and humble in heart, and you will find rest for your souls. For my yoke is easy and my burden is light.*

Jesus was using an illustration from everyday life in the first century. When a young ox was being broken in and trained, it was harnessed (yoked) to a lead ox. The lead ox knew the ropes. It knew that the best way to finish a day's work was neither to sit nor run. The lead ox knew that they would get the job done if they walked down the narrow row, looking neither to the right nor to the left. And if the oxen were going to effectively finish the work, they would have to do it together.

The young ox, however, would often get impatient with the slow, steady pace and would want to run ahead. What do you think he got? A stiff neck!

Sometimes the young ox would get tired or hot and so he'd sit and refuse to budge. What do you think he got then? You guessed it—another stiff neck.

The lead ox would keep on walking, because life goes on whether we like it or not. You can count on Jesus—like that wise lead ox—to lead you in a steady pace down the center of that narrow path of God's will. And He will steady the pace so you do not become exhausted and quit.

My (Neil) family's second dog, Buster, was a disaster. He

grew up to be a true D-A-W-G! He is the most neurotic mess I've ever seen. My son, Karl, signed up for twelve dog-obedience lessons with Buster. But after just two weeks it was Karl who was thoroughly trained by the dog!

I tried putting a choke chain around Buster's neck and taking him for a walk. I wanted that dog to know one thing: I was the master, and I was going to decide where we were going and how fast we would go to get there! Buster, however, wanted to run. He would strain at the end of the leash and cough and choke all the way through our "walk." Buster also wanted to stop at every tree, fire hydrant, bush, or blade of grass on the way. But I wanted to keep walking. I would have to literally drag the hacking dog along.

Sometimes he would stray off the path and end up winding his leash around a tree. The result was like a wild ride at an amusement park, but I kept on walking.

Did that dumb dog ever learn to walk obediently by my side? No, he never did. And for all his pains all he got was—you guessed it—a stiff neck! Unfortunately, many Christians are just like that—stubborn, self-willed, and stiff-necked!

Jesus said that we would find rest if we take His yoke upon us. How can a yoke be comfortable? If the other part of the team is a good leader. And you can only put on Jesus' light and easy yoke after you throw off every other one you might be wearing.

What are some common yokes? Trying to fit in with the crowd at school. Trying to keep up with the latest fads. Trying to be perfect in everything you do. Trying to please God by religious activity. Trying to excel at something so that someone will finally notice you and accept you.

Isn't it time to stop running the show yourself? Isn't it time to learn from Jesus that our walk through life is by faith and not by sight? Isn't it time to start living according to the truth that you are already loved and accepted by God through grace and not by works?

Wouldn't it be great to find rest for your soul? Then get rid of any yoke of slavery that is dragging you down and wearing you out. Let Jesus lead. He is gentle and humble in heart.

We are not only to walk by the Spirit, but we are to be led by the Spirit as well. Being led means we are neither being driven (legalism) or lured away (license).

There are a lot of driven Christians who know very little about resting in the Spirit. Motivated by guilt or fear, they can't say no. They use up a lot of energy but bear little fruit. They are busy but not truly productive for the kingdom of God.

Other believers are being led astray by deceiving spirits. Undisciplined and lazy, they don't want to take time to study what God says, so they try to take a shortcut. They end up listening to spirit guides who tempt them with promises of special or secret knowledge and power.

We are to be led by the Spirit of God, and He is the Spirit of truth who will guide us into the truth as we learn to listen to His voice.

Speaking of Animals _____

Growing up on a farm, I (Neil) had the privilege of raising championship sheep. I can tell you from experience that sheep are not the smartest animals on the farm! For instance, you can allow pigs and cattle to eat as much as they want because they have the sense to stop when they are full. But not sheep! If you turn sheep loose in a green pasture, they will literally eat themselves to death.

One thing is certain: Sheep without a shepherd are in big, big trouble!

In the Western world, we drive our sheep from the rear,

much like the Australians who use sheepdogs. However, that is not the case in Israel. In my trips to the Holy Land, I noticed that herds of sheep were usually small, and a shepherd watched over them.

The shepherd sat patiently while the flock grazed. He seemed to know each sheep personally and have a real love for them. When an area was sufficiently grazed, the shepherd would say something and walk off. To my amazement, the sheep all looked up and followed him.

What a beautiful picture of what the Lord Jesus said in John 10:27: "My sheep listen to my voice; I know them, and they follow me."

Walking by the Spirit is neither license nor legalism. It is liberty, and it is listening to the voice of the Shepherd. It is not passively sitting around doing nothing nor anxiously running around trying to do everything. It is a walk of faith: "For we walk by faith, not by sight" (2 Cor. 5:7 NASB).

Walking by the Spirit means neither being driven nor lured off the path of faith. It means being led, "because those who are led by the Spirit of God are sons of God" (Rom. 8:14).

Walking by the Spirit is walking with God. It is recognizing that Jesus is the vine and you are a branch. It is choosing to depend on that vine for all that you need, realizing that apart from Christ you can do nothing (John 15:5). It is realizing, however, that you can do all things through Christ who strengthens you (Phil. 4:13).

Would you join us as we pray for the freedom that comes from keeping pace with God, hand in hand with His Spirit?

Dear heavenly Father, You are the strength of my life. Forgive me for trying to live by my own strength and resources. I not only need Your power, but I need Your wise guidance as well. I accept the times that You put me in a "holding pattern" in my life. I recog-

nize that You always work for Your glory and my good. Teach me to listen for and trust in Your voice. Right now I choose to throw off every yoke that is a burden to me. I gladly accept the yoke of Jesus. I reject license and legalism. I want to walk in true liberty. Thank You, Jesus, that You have promised that I will find rest for my soul as I walk with You.

I commit myself to learning from You through Your Word, so I can be guided by Your Spirit. I reject the influence of any and all deceiving spirits that seek to lead me astray. I renounce all leaning on my own understanding.

Lord, I need Your wisdom, and most of all, I need You. Please fill me with Your Holy Spirit so that I can follow Jesus, the Good Shepherd. Thank You for the security that comes from walking with You. Amen.

Prayer: Our Lifeline and Hot Line to the Father

President John F. Kennedy was a busy man. It was the nature of his job. Like most presidents he spent endless hours in meetings, traveling, and talking on the phone. But President Kennedy was also a family man.

His son, John-John (now John F. Kennedy, Jr.) was a young boy during those years in the White House. Any time—day or night—John-John had complete clearance to see his dad. Even if President Kennedy was in an important meeting, his son could race past all the security guards, burst into the Oval Office, and hop up into his daddy's lap.

The rights and privileges that John-John enjoyed with the most powerful man in America were granted to him because he was the child of the president. No one could keep that little boy from spending time with his daddy, except John-

John himself. The door was always wide open for him to talk to his father, but the choice to go through that door was John-John's to make. And he did!

When it comes to prayer—listening to and talking with our heavenly Father—all of us would agree that it is crucial to a close walk with God. After all, how can we possibly know God's will without knowing God? And how can we get to know the Father if we are not spending time with Him? Yet there is probably no greater area of frustration for the average Christian young person than this area of prayer. Most of us have great intentions, but after just a few minutes of rattling off our prayer requests, we're often at a loss for words.

How can we develop the kind of closeness to our heavenly Father that causes us to spend unhurried time with Him? Is it possible for a teenager to be so close to God that the following words of the psalmist are echoed in his or her heart as well?: "As the deer pants for streams of water, so my soul pants for you, O God. / My soul thirsts for God, for the living God. / When can I go and meet with God?" (Ps. 42:1-2).

It is more than possible. It is God's will! In fact, Proverbs 15:8 tells us that "the prayer of the upright is His delight" (NASB). Isn't that incredible? God gets psyched when we spend time with Him! It brings joy to His heart to talk with His precious children! Why? Because He loves us and we are His pride and joy, "the apple of his eye" (Zech. 2:8).

Perhaps for you the words *father* and *daddy* don't give you any warm fuzzies. Therefore, it's hard for you to get excited about "hopping up into your heavenly Father's lap."

It's easy to fall into the trap of assuming that our Father in heaven is just like our dad on earth. That is simply not the case. No dad on earth is perfect, but our heavenly Father is. He is the Father you have always needed and wanted.

In order to experience freedom and closeness in your prayer life, you will need to renounce (verbally reject) any lies that you have believed about your Father in heaven. And then you need to choose to believe the truth about Him. Once you do that, you will find that "spiritual wall" between yourself and God torn down.

The following exercise is designed to help you do just that. It is important that you read it *out loud*. Work your way down the list, starting with the first statement on the left: *I renounce the lie that my heavenly Father is distant and disinterested*. Then read the corresponding statement on the right: *I joyfully accept the truth that my heavenly Father is intimate and involved*. And continue on down the list.

The Truth about My Heavenly Father

I renounce the lie that my heavenly Father is:	*I joyfully accept the truth that my heavenly Father is:*
1. distant and disinterested.	1. intimate and involved.
2. insensitive and uncaring.	2. kind and compassionate.
3. stern, demanding, or perfectionistic.	3. accepting and filled with joyful love.
4. passive and cold.	4. warm and affectionate.
5. absent or too busy for me.	5. always with me and always eager to spend time with me.
6. never satisfied with what I do; impatient or angry.	6. patient, slow to anger, and pleased with me in Christ.

7. mean, cruel, or abusive.

8. trying to take all the fun out of life.

9. controlling or manipulative.

10. condemning or unforgiving.

7. loving, gentle, and protective of me.

8. trustworthy, and He wants to give me life to the full. His will is good, perfect, and acceptable for me.

9. full of grace and mercy, giving me the freedom to fail.

10. tenderhearted, forgiving, with His heart and arms always open to me.

I am the apple of His eye!

Praying in the Spirit

I (Neil) reached a turning point in my life when I had to prepare a series of lessons on prayer. The last one was "How to Pray in the Spirit." The night before I was to give that final message, I became painfully aware of a problem: I was clueless about how to pray in the Spirit!

Only hours away from "show time" I poured out my heart to God. I was running on spiritual "empty," and that was exactly where He wanted me to be. Sometime before midnight the Lord began to direct my thoughts through the Bible. It was one of the most important nights of my life.

At first I turned to Ephesians 5:18-20. I figured, *If I'm going to pray in the Spirit, I must be filled with the Spirit.* The passage in Ephesians opened my eyes:

Be filled with the Spirit, speaking to one another in psalms and hymns and spiritual songs, singing and making melody with your heart to the Lord; always giving thanks for all things in the name of our Lord Jesus Christ to God, even the Father. (NASB)

Then I flipped over to a similar passage in Colossians 3:15-17:

Let the peace of Christ rule in your hearts, to which indeed you were called in one body; and be thankful. Let the word of Christ richly dwell within you, with all wisdom teaching and admonishing one another with psalms and hymns and spiritual songs, singing with thankfulness in your hearts to God. And whatever you do in word or deed, do all in the name of the Lord Jesus, giving thanks through Him to God the Father. (NASB)

I noticed that being filled with the Spirit and letting the Word of Christ richly dwell within me were tied in closely with giving thanks. So I looked ahead to Colossians 4:2: "Devote yourselves to prayer, keeping alert in it with an attitude of thanksgiving" (NASB).

Now, if that isn't a helpful bit of advice on prayer, I don't know what is! Do you want to keep from having your mind drift off in your prayers? Give thanks!

I continued and read 1 Thessalonians 5:16-18: "Rejoice always; pray without ceasing; in everything give thanks; for this is God's will for you in Christ Jesus" (NASB). Do you want to know God's will for you in prayer? According to this passage and the two that preceded it, the instruction is clear: Have a rejoicing heart. Both the Ephesians 5 and Colossians 3 passages quoted above talked about that too! Let songs of praise come from your heart and your lips to God. And give thanks!

Try this as an experiment and see if you don't have a great time talking with your Father: Spend an unhurried time giving thanks to God for everything you can think of. Start with things you usually take for granted like air to breathe, clothes to keep you warm, food and water, etc. Nothing is too trivial to thank Him for. You can say "thank you" to God for the trees, grass, birds, flowers, clouds, rain, wind, snow, and so on. You name it, you can give thanks for it! Why? Because it is God's will for us to give thanks to Him *in everything*.

Singing praises to God and giving thanks from your heart are two surefire ways to add zip to your prayer life. Perhaps the most important ingredient in your prayer life is an *attitude of gratitude*. Hebrews 13:15 puts it this way: "Through Him [Jesus] then, let us continually offer up a sacrifice of praise to God, that is, the fruit of lips that give thanks to His name" (NASB).

But we are not just to give thanks for *things*; we are to give thanks for *people* as well. So when you begin praying for others, start by giving thanks. That's how the apostle Paul prayed, as the following Bible verses show:

- [I] do not cease giving thanks for you, while making mention of you in my prayers. (Eph. 1:16 NASB)
- We give thanks to God, the Father of our Lord Jesus Christ, praying always for you. (Col. 1:3 NASB)
- First of all, then, I urge that entreaties and prayers, petitions and thanksgivings, be made on behalf of all men. (1 Tim. 2:1 NASB)

There are other examples of Paul's thankful praying as well. But why is giving thanks in prayer so important when you are praying for people? It is because our *hearts* must be right before our *prayers* will be right. And when you are finally able to honestly give thanks for someone, then you are ready to pray for him or her!

That same important night in my life, I turned to Romans 8:26–27:

In the same way, the Spirit helps us in our weakness. We do not know what we ought to pray for, but the Spirit himself intercedes for us with groans that words cannot express. And he who searches our hearts knows the mind of the Spirit, because the Spirit intercedes for the saints in accordance with God's will.

It may come as a shock (or relief!) to you to know that none of us really knows what to pray for. But the Spirit of God does! How does the Holy Spirit help us pray? I wasn't sure, but I tried something that evening. I said, "Okay, Lord, I'm setting aside my prayer list, and I'm going to assume that whatever comes to my mind during this prayer time is from You or allowed by You. I'm going to let You direct me."

And that's what I did. Whatever came to my mind that evening is what I prayed about. If I had a tempting thought, I talked to God about that area of weakness in my life. If all the things I had to do came to mind, I discussed my plans with God.

Don't get me wrong. I wasn't passively letting thoughts control me. I was actively taking every thought captive to the obedience of Christ (2 Cor. 10:5). Be careful! If you become lazy in your thinking, you can easily end up paying attention to a deceiving spirit (1 Tim. 4:1).

If my mind entertained a lying or evil thought, I didn't ignore it. I brought it up before the Lord. Usually such a thought identifies an area of weakness or unconfessed sin that we need to get real with God about. God will sometimes allow us to be mentally jerked around by the devil until we finally bring our struggles before the only One who can take care of them.

I think that's why Scripture teaches in several places, including Hebrews 4:7: "Today if you hear His voice, / do not harden your hearts" (NASB).

There are basically only two responses to the Word of God and the leading of the Spirit of God—you can *harden* your heart or *open* your heart.

In my personal prayer life, I had been trying to shove away evil thoughts, but without much success. But when I brought them into the light and got honest with God, it was amazing how much freedom I found!

All the issues I was trying to ignore during prayer were exactly the issues God wanted me to deal with. Once you start being open, honest, and real with God, you'll discover how real and personal He is. That's why Scripture promises us: "Draw near to God and He will draw near to you" (James 4:8 NASB).

Sadly, too many Christians never experience that kind of closeness to their heavenly Father. Many are "too busy" to pray. Others are so busy trying to "act spiritual" with God that they never get real. Come on, God already knows what's going on in your life, and He loves you just the same. Isn't it time to knock off the "spiritual" act and just be yourself with Him?

It's Called Fellowship

Fellowship with God involves a living, loving, open relationship with Him. God doesn't expect us to be perfect, just honest. John calls this walking "in the light as He Himself is in the light" (1 John 1:7 NASB).

How is it possible to be this open with God? We are His children. We don't have to pretend with God in hopes that He will accept us. As His kids, we're already accepted completely in Christ!

You may, however, find yourself feeling uncomfortable

in His presence. That would be understandable if you are unwilling to let God be God in your life. He is a Father who loves you too much to let you ruin your life in rebellion and disobedience. And He is certainly not going to be interested in listening to a list of selfish demands disguised as "prayer requests."

Remember that God is on your side. He loves you and has already proven that point by making the ultimate sacrifice—the death of His Son—for you. Don't let your enemy, Satan, fake you out and make you think God is your enemy. Nothing could be farther from the truth, as Hebrews 4:15-16 shows:

> For we do not have a high priest who is unable to sympathize with our weaknesses, but we have one [Jesus] who has been tempted in every way, just as we are—yet was without sin. Let us then approach the throne of grace with confidence, so that we may receive mercy and find grace to help us in our time of need.

When I (Rich) was a kid, I wanted every animal I saw on TV as a pet. If I saw a Walt Disney show on raccoons, I wanted a raccoon. If I saw one on wolves, I wanted a wolf. I watched the old *Flipper* shows and wanted a dolphin. But the animal I wanted the most was a horse. I thought Mr. Ed was really cool!

I had no idea how much money a horse cost. I only knew that it was a lot more than I had. So one day I plotted to get some horse money.

Every Thursday night my dad would get paid and come home with a big wad of money ... which he would promptly turn over to Mom! One such night, while my parents were in the living room watching TV, I sneaked over to Mom's purse. There, as expected, was that wad of twenty-dollar bills.

"They'll never miss one of them," I said to myself, and I plucked one out.

In order to trick my parents, I came up with a brilliant idea. That weekend I went down to the woods where I played, taking the twenty-dollar bill and an envelope with me. I put the money in the envelope and rubbed it around in the dirt, making it look like it had been there for a while. Then I ran home, burst in the door, and announced my discovery.

"Look, Mom, Dad, I found this envelope in the woods and it has $20 in it!" I deserved an Oscar for my performance, I thought.

"That's great, Rich. You can use that money toward your horse!" My mom was excited for me and was playing right into my hands. Things could not have been better.

But as the day went on, my conscience began to bother me more and more. I started feeling really guilty for stealing from and lying to my parents.

In the evening I had Little League baseball practice. After practice was over, I started walking over toward my dad, who was sitting on a little hill watching me play and waiting for me to finish. The closer I got to him, the worse I felt. By the time I reached my dad, I was crying.

"I didn't find that money in the woods. I stole it!" I sobbed.

"Your mother and I knew you had stolen that money, son," he assured me as he hugged me.

I couldn't believe it! The crime of the century had been solved even before my confession? That made me feel even worse and my crying shifted into third gear. "You knew?" I asked in disbelief.

"Yes, son, we knew. We were just waiting for you to come and tell us."

Well, that did it. I slammed into overdrive in the tears department as all the guilt and fear were gone. I was sorry,

I had owned up to what I had done, and they loved me anyway.

Years later as I think about that incident, I am reminded of the words of the apostle John when he wrote:

This is the message we have heard from him and declare to you: God is light; in him there is no darkness at all. If we claim to have fellowship with him yet walk in the darkness, we lie and do not live by the truth. But if we walk in the light, as he is in the light, we have fellowship with one another, and the blood of Jesus, his Son, purifies us from all sin. If we claim to be without sin, we deceive ourselves and the truth is not in us. If we confess our sins, he is faithful and just and will forgive us our sins and purify us from all unrighteousness. (1 John 1:5-9)

Jesus told a parable (a teaching story) to let us know how the Father feels about us when we sin and how He reacts when we own up to what we've done. It's found in Luke 15, and we recommend you read it.

The story is about two brothers. The older one was loyal to his dad, worked hard, and caused no real trouble. The younger one was different. He was sick and tired of "life on the farm," so he decided to take some action.

One day he went up to his dad and asked for his inheritance money so he could go and taste life in the big city. His dad gave it to him, and the boy took off to find fame and fortune.

The kid lived it up. He spent his money on all the things he used to just dream of doing—booze, women, the whole works. But then his money ran out, and times got tough. To make matters worse, there was a famine in the land and the unemployment rate was running high.

To make ends meet, the boy got a job feeding pigs, which was about as low as a Jewish kid could go in those days.

Today, that would compare to cleaning the toilets in a downtown New York City subway station in the middle of summer.

Finally, Jesus said, the boy "came to his senses." He looked at the pea pods the pigs were eating, wishing he could eat them too, and suddenly it dawned on him: His dad's hired hands had it better than he did, and he was his son! At that moment he decided to go home.

On his way home he rehearsed the speech he would give his dad. It went something like, "Dad, I've really blown it—sinning against God and you. I don't even deserve to be called your son anymore. I'll gladly work for you as a hired hand."

While the boy was still a long way off, however, his dad spotted him. He leaped out of his chair, flew out the door, and raced down the driveway to meet him. Before the boy could say a word, the dad had thrown his arms around him and kissed him.

The kid tried to give his speech, but Dad wasn't listening. He told his servants to put his best robe on his son, as well as a ring on his hand and sandals on his feet.

Then they threw a party to end all parties, because in his dad's words, "This son of mine was dead, and has come to life again; he was lost, and has been found" (Luke 15:24 NASB).

Did you catch it? The boy's dad wasn't standing in the driveway, arms folded, tapping his foot impatiently. He didn't scold the boy, saying, "It's about time you got home, you deadbeat!"

Nor was Dad out in the field somewhere working. He didn't turn his back on the kid when he saw him coming and give him the silent treatment.

What was the father doing? He was waiting, looking, hoping, longing for the return of his son.

So why did Jesus tell this parable? Remember, it was to

show us how our heavenly Father feels about us. It was to remind us that no matter what we've done or where we've been or how long we've been gone, we can always go home.

It is always okay to come home.

If your desire is to develop that kind of warm, open, personal relationship with your heavenly Father, then feel free to join us as we pray.

Dear heavenly Father, I thank You for the incredible opportunity that I have to talk to You any time of the day or night, every day of my life. Forgive me for the times I was too busy to talk with You. Forgive me for the times I tried to pretend I was more spiritual than I was.

I choose right now to walk in the light with You, being honest and open about how I feel and what I think.

Create in me a heart that is filled with praise and thanksgiving to You for who You are and what You have done. Teach me how to pray, for I don't know how to pray as I should. I lay aside my own ideas and choose to let You instruct me through Your Word and Your Spirit.

Thank You that I can always come home to You and find Your arms and heart open wide. I am Your child and nothing can ever change that. Because You know best, I trust my entire life to You. Amen.

CHAPTER 15

The
Parable
of the Car

There was a time not too long ago when few people had cars. Most people walked wherever they had to go, because walking was safe and walkers prided themselves on how strong their legs were.

Some folks had cars, but since most people were suspicious of those "new-fangled gadgets," many of the drivers kept their cars locked up in their garages so no one would think they were weird. They would bring them out on Sunday, but they would lock them up again during the rest of the week.

Generally, it was not considered polite to talk about cars. It tended to make walkers nervous when the subject of "cars" was brought up, and most drivers were very careful not to offend anyone who did not have a car.

One day a teenager named David was walking to school, as he always did. He had been watching some of the cars zip by and thinking about how tired he was. Suddenly, one of his friends pulled up alongside and asked him if he wanted a ride. His other friends, who were walking with him, warned him not to do it and poked fun at the driver. But David was curious.

"Okay, I'll ride with you, but just this once," David said for the benefit of his walker-friends. There was a friendly looking man sitting up front in the passenger seat, so David opened the door and climbed in the backseat.

"Who's your buddy?" David asked his friend.

"Oh, he's the owner of the car," his driver-friend replied. "He goes with me wherever I drive. He comes with the car, or rather, the car comes with him. He is teaching me how to drive and shows me the best places to go and how to get there."

This seemed very strange to David, since he was used to walking wherever he or his friends wanted to go. But he had to admit, his driver-friend sure seemed happy and a lot less tired than he was. So he sat back and watched the two talk.

Many times the man would read from the Owner's Manual of the car. David couldn't understand most of it, but his driver-friend seemed to find the information very helpful to his driving.

Finally, David asked his friend how he got his car.

"He gave it to me to use," the driver said, pointing at the man in the front seat.

"He *gave* it to you?"

"That's right. And he'll give you one too. On two conditions."

"What conditions?"

"One, you have to let him go with you wherever you go. By the way, that isn't so hard. Once you get to know him, you wouldn't want to go anywhere or do anything without him."

"Okay, he seems nice enough. What's the other condition?" David asked excitedly.

"You have to be willing to become a *driver* instead of a *walker.*"

"But all my friends are walkers."

"Yeah, that's true, David. But all your friends are tired too."

David thought about the deal and finally agreed. His friend immediately drove him to the new car lot and David spied the car he wanted. When he opened the door and climbed into the driver's seat, it seemed like it had been made just for him. And much to his amazement, that kind man was sitting next to him smiling.

So off they drove. Driving seemed so easy. The man showed him how to steer. He taught him about road signs and why they should be obeyed. He warned him of dangers and took him on trips to see beautiful places.

One day the man told him to drive to school.

"Drive to school? Are you out of your mind?" David asked, shocked. "All my friends will think I'm crazy!"

"Did you think your driver-friend was crazy?" the man asked quietly.

"Yes. I mean, well, a little. At first, anyway. But you don't understand. My friends can't handle this yet. It's all too new. No, today wouldn't be a good time for this at all. Tomorrow would be much better. Yeah, I'll drive to school tomorrow, okay?"

The man fell silent as David took off down the road, toward the beautiful mountains they had seen yesterday. As they drove they passed strange-looking buildings where drivers seemed to be putting some kind of liquid into their cars. The man kept gently encouraging David to stop and pull in.

"Not today, sir! I don't have time for that. We've got to get to the mountains and back before dark. Maybe tomorrow."

The man became very quiet once again.

David flipped on the radio so he wouldn't feel so alone. There were many stations to choose from. Some stations had interesting speakers giving driving tips from the Owner's Manual. Then there would be songs about the importance of stopping at service stations.

"Humph. Stupid commercials," David muttered as he changed the station.

He finally found some music that he liked. Some of the songs talked about all the great things walkers could do. Other songs warned him not to listen to anyone but himself. He began to think about all that he was missing, now that he was a driver.

After driving for a few hours, the car started acting funny. They were well up in the mountains by now, with few other cars around. As the car ground to a halt, David asked the man what was wrong. He seemed to be asleep. David was angry at the car and at the man.

He got out, slammed the door, and looked under the hood as he had seen others do, but he had no idea what to look for.

"I'm not getting anywhere this way," David grumbled to himself. "Hey, can you help me push this stupid thing?" he yelled at the man. But he got no response.

So he started pushing the car back toward home. Every once in a while he would pass another driver pushing his car. They would kind of smile at each other bravely and hurry on their way. Some of the pushing drivers told David that they had been doing this for years. They looked very tired. David wondered if they even remembered what actually driving the car was like.

Every once in a while David would pass one of the service

stations and friendly people there would shout greetings of encouragement to drop in. Some told him that his car was out of gas, and they could help him fill up again.

"It's all written right there in the Owner's Manual," one of them said.

"Sorry, not today. I'm too busy. Maybe tomorrow." David said as he pushed on.

The hardest part was having to endure the laughter and pointing fingers of the walkers he passed. David wished that he had never become a driver at all. He was more tired than ever. And now it was getting dark, and he was a little scared.

Finally, when David was at the point of exhaustion, a fellow driver pulled up and got out of his car.

"Hey, buddy, you really look worn out. What's going on?"

"I'm trying to get home," David told him.

"Well, listen, don't you realize that your car has an engine in it? It has a lot more power than you do."

"Yeah, I know. It was great at first, but I just can't figure out how to get it going again." David was almost in tears as he looked into the other driver's sympathetic eyes.

"I know exactly what you mean. I pushed my car for years before I realized I needed to take the time and stop at a service station and fill up with gasoline."

David couldn't believe what he was hearing. "Oh, I've been so stupid. The man who owns my car kept telling me that, but I wouldn't listen."

"Yeah, neither did I. Listen, don't be a jerk like I was. Let me help push you into that service station up ahead. And by the way, if you tell the owner how foolish you've been and tell him you want to listen to what he has to say again, I think he might just help us."

The two drivers had been so busy talking that they had not noticed David's car was already halfway to the service station. The owner had quietly slipped out of his seat and begun pushing for them.

"Hey, wait up!" David yelled, the tears streaming down his face. "You don't have to do that by yourself. Let me help."

David ran as fast as he could to catch up with the man. When he reached him he was out of breath. "Sir, I have been so busy listening to me that I stopped listening to you. Will you forgive me?"

The man smiled. "You can call me Jesus, my brother. Now, will you stop yakking and start pushing? We've got to get you home so you can be ready to drive to school tomorrow. Right?"

"Oh, yeah. I did say that, didn't I?" David looked sheepish.

"Yes, you did."

"You'll go with me?" David asked hopefully.

"I went with you today, didn't I?"

David nodded.

"David, my dear friend, the question is never whether I will go with you. I will never leave you or desert you. The question is, will you go with Me?"

Steps to Freedom in Christ

Spiritual freedom is meant for every Christian, young or old. But what does it mean to be "free in Christ"? It is to have the desire and power to worship God and do His will. It is to know God's truth, believe God's truth, and live according to God's truth. Being free in Christ means release from the chains of the sins of our past, problems of the present, and fears of the future. It is to walk with God in the power of the Holy Spirit and to experience a life of love, joy, and peace. It is not a life of perfection, but progress! All these qualities may not be yours now, but they are meant for everyone who is in Christ.

If you have received Christ as your Savior, He has already set you free through His victory over sin and death on the cross. But if freedom is not a constant reality for you, it may be because you do not understand how Christ can help you deal with the pain of your past or the problems of your present life. It is your responsibility as one who knows Christ to do whatever is needed to maintain a right relationship with God. Your eternal life is not at stake; you are safe and secure in Christ. But you will not experience all that Christ has for you if you fail to understand who you are in Christ and fail to live according to that truth.

We've got great news for you! You may be young, but you are not a helpless victim caught between two nearly equal but opposite heavenly superpowers, God and Satan. Only God is all-powerful, always present, and all-knowing. Sometimes, however, the presence and power of sin and evil in our lives can seem more real to us than the presence and power of God. But that is part of Satan's tricky lie. Satan is a deceiver, and he wants you to think he is stronger than he really is. But he is also a defeated enemy, and you are in Christ, the Victor. Understanding who God is and who you are in Christ are the two most important factors in determining your daily victory over sin and Satan. False beliefs about God, not understanding who you are as a child of God, and making Satan out to be as powerful and present as God are the greatest causes of spiritual defeat.

The battle is for your mind. You may experience nagging thoughts like, "This isn't going to work," or "God doesn't love me." These thoughts are lies, implanted in your mind by deceiving spirits. If you believe them, you will really struggle as you work through these steps. These opposing thoughts can control you only if you believe them.

If you are working through these steps by yourself, don't pay attention to any lying or threatening thoughts in your mind. If you're working through the steps with a trusted friend, youth pastor, parent, or counselor (which we strongly recommend), then share any opposing thoughts with that person. Whenever you uncover a lie and choose to believe the truth, the power of Satan is broken.

As believers in Christ, we can pray with authority to stop any interference by Satan. Here is a prayer and declaration to get you started. Read them (and all prayers and declarations in these steps) out loud.

Dear heavenly Father, we know that You are always here and present in our lives. You are the only all-knowing, all-powerful, ever-present God. We desperately need You, because without Jesus we can do nothing. We believe the Bible because it tells us what is really true. We refuse to believe the lies of Satan. We stand in the truth that all authority in heaven and on earth has been given to the resurrected Christ. Because we are in Christ, we share His authority in order to make followers of Jesus and set captives free. We ask You to protect our thoughts and minds and lead us into all truth. We choose to submit to the Holy Spirit. Please reveal to our minds everything You want to deal with today. We ask for and trust in Your wisdom. We pray for Your complete protection over us. In Jesus' name. Amen.

Declaration

In the name and the authority of the Lord Jesus Christ, we command Satan and all evil spirits to let go of (name) in order that (name) can be free to know and choose to do the will of God. As children of God, seated with Christ in the heavenlies, we agree that every enemy of the Lord Jesus Christ be bound and gagged to silence. We say to Satan and all of his evil workers that you cannot inflict any pain or in any way stop or hinder God's will from being done today in (name) life.

Following are seven steps that can free you from your past. You will cover the areas where Satan most often takes advantage of us and where strongholds have been built. Christ purchased your victory when He shed His blood for you on the cross. You will experience your freedom when you make the choice to believe, confess, forgive, renounce, and forsake. No one can do that for you. The battle for your mind can only be won as you personally choose truth.

As you go through these Steps to Freedom in Christ, remember that Satan cannot read your mind, thus he won't obey your thoughts. Only God knows what you are thinking. As you go through each step, it is important that you submit to God inwardly and resist the devil by reading each prayer out loud—verbally renouncing, forgiving, confessing, etc.

You are going to take a thorough look at your life in order to get radically right with God. It may turn out that you have another kind of problem (not covered in these steps) which is negatively affecting your life. But if you are open and honest during this time, you will greatly benefit by becoming right with God and close to Him again.

May the Lord greatly touch your life during this time. He will give you the strength to make it through. It is essential that you work through all seven steps, so don't allow yourself to become discouraged and give up. Remember, the freedom that Christ purchased for all believers on the cross is meant for *you!*

Step 1: Counterfeit Versus Real _____

The first step toward experiencing your freedom in Christ is to renounce (to reject and turn your back on all past, present, and future involvement with) any participation in Satan-inspired occult practices, things done in secret, and non-Christian religions. You must renounce any activity and group which denies Jesus Christ, offers direction through any source other than the absolute authority of the written Word of God, or requires secret initiations, ceremonies, promises, or pacts (covenants). Begin with the following prayer:

Dear heavenly Father, I ask You to reveal to me anything that I have done or that someone has done to me that is spiritually wrong. Reveal to my mind any and all involvement I have knowingly or unknowingly had with cult or occult practices, and/or false teachers. I want to experience Your freedom and do only Your will. I ask this in Jesus' name. Amen.

Even if you took part in something as a game or as a joke, you need to renounce it. Satan will try to take advantage of anything he can in our lives. Even if you just stood by and watched others do it, you need to renounce it. Even if you did it just once and had no idea it was evil, still you need to renounce it. You want to remove any and every possible foothold of Satan in your life.

Non-Christian Spiritual Checklist
(Please check all those that apply to you)

☐ Out-of-body experience (astral travel)
☐ Mormonism (Latter-Day Saints)
☐ Ouija board
☐ Jehovah Witness
☐ Bloody Mary
☐ New Age

☐ *Light as a Feather* (or other occult games)
☐ New Age medicine
☐ Masons
☐ Magic Eight Ball
☐ Christian Science
☐ Table lifting or body lifting

- ☐ Science of the Mind
- ☐ Using spells or curses
- ☐ Science of Creative Intelligence
- ☐ Attempting to control others by putting thoughts in their head
- ☐ The Way International
- ☐ Automatic writing
- ☐ Unification Church (Moonies)
- ☐ Spirit guides
- ☐ Fortunetelling
- ☐ The Forum (EST)
- ☐ Tarot cards
- ☐ Church of the Living Word
- ☐ Palm reading
- ☐ Astrology/Horoscopes
- ☐ Children of God (Children of Love)
- ☐ Hypnosis
- ☐ Black or white magic
- ☐ Seances
- ☐ Dungeons & Dragons (or other fantasy role-playing games)
- ☐ Scientology
- ☐ Unitarianism
- ☐ Video or computer games involving occult powers or cruel violence
- ☐ Roy Masters
- ☐ Silva Mind Control
- ☐ Blood pacts or cutting yourself on purpose
- ☐ Transcendental Meditation (TM)
- ☐ Objects of worship/ crystals/good luck charms
- ☐ Yoga
- ☐ Hare Krishna
- ☐ Sexual spirits
- ☐ Bahaism
- ☐ Martial Arts (involving Eastern mysticism meditation or devotion to sensei)
- ☐ Native American Spirit Worship
- ☐ Idols of rock stars, actors/actresses, sports heroes, etc.
- ☐ Buddhism (including Zen)
- ☐ Rosicrucianism
- ☐ Islam
- ☐ Hinduism
- ☐ Black Muslim

NOTE: This is not a complete list. If you have any doubts about an activity not included here, renounce your involvement in it. If it has come to mind here, trust that the Lord wants you to renounce it.

Anti-Christian Movies

_____

_____

_____

Anti-Christian Music

_____

_____

_____

Anti-Christian TV Shows or Video Games

_____

_____

_____

Anti-Christian Books, Magazines, or Comics

_____

_____

_____

1. Have you ever heard or seen or felt a spiritual being in your room?
2. Have you had an imaginary friend that talked to you?
3. Have you ever heard voices in your head or had repeating negative, nagging thoughts such as "I'm dumb," "I'm ugly," "Nobody loves me," "I can't do anything right," etc. as if a conversation were going on in your head? Explain.
4. Have you or anyone in your family ever consulted a medium, spiritist, or channeler? If yes, who?
5. What other spiritual experiences have you had that would be considered out of the ordinary (telepathy, speaking in a trance, known something supernaturally, contact with aliens, etc.)?
6. Have you ever been involved in satanic worship of any kind or attended a concert at which Satan was the focus?
7. Have you ever made a vow or pact?

Once you have completed the above checklist, confess and renounce each item you were involved in by praying aloud the following prayer (repeat the prayer separately for each item on your list):

Lord, I confess that I have participated in _____. I thank You for Your forgiveness and I renounce any and all influence and involvement with _____.

If you have been involved in any satanic rituals or heavy occult activity (or you suspect it because of blocked memories, severe and recurring nightmares, or sexual bondage), you need to say out loud the following special renunciations and affirmations.

Read across the page, renouncing the first item in the column under *Domain of Darkness* and then affirming the first truth in the column under *Kingdom of Light*. Continue down the entire list in that manner.

Domain of Darkness	*Kingdom of Light*
1. I renounce ever signing my name over to Satan or having my name signed over to Satan by someone else.	1. I announce that my name is now written in the Lamb's Book of Life.
2. I renounce any ceremony in which I was wed to Satan.	2. I announce that I am the Bride of Christ.
3. I renounce any and all covenants, agreements, or promises that I made with Satan.	3. I announce that I have a new covenant with Jesus Christ alone.

4. I renounce all satanic assignments for my life, including duties, marriage, and children.

5. I renounce all spirit guides assigned to me.

6. I renounce ever giving of my blood in the service of Satan.

7. I renounce ever eating flesh or drinking blood in satanic worship.

8. I renounce all guardians and satanic parents that were assigned to me.

9. I renounce any baptism whereby I am identified with Satan.

10. I renounce every sacrifice made on my behalf by which Satan may claim ownership of me.

4. I announce and commit myself to know and do only the will of God, and I accept only His guidance for my life.

5. I announce and accept only the leading of the Holy Spirit.

6. I trust only in the shed blood of my Lord Jesus Christ.

7. By faith I eat only the flesh and drink only the blood of the Lord Jesus in Holy Communion.

8. I announce that God is my Heavenly Father and the Holy Spirit is my guardian by whom I am sealed.

9. I announce that I have been baptized into Christ Jesus and my identity is now in Him.

10. I announce that only the sacrifice of Christ has any claim on me. I belong to Him. I have been purchased by the blood of the Lamb.

Step 2: Deception Versus Truth _____

God's Word is true, and we need to accept the truth deep in our hearts (Ps. 51:6). When King David lived a lie, he really suffered. When he finally found freedom by admitting that he'd sinned, he wrote, "Blessed is the man . . . in whose spirit is no deceit" (Ps. 32:2). We must stop lying to ourselves and to each other and speak the truth in love (Eph. 4:15, 25). Mentally healthy young people can face the truth, live in a real world, and not let fear control them. Scripture tells us that God is the only one we should fear. This means that we hold Him in highest respect and are in great awe of His power, majesty, and holiness.

Start this important step by praying the following prayer out loud. Don't let opposing thoughts such as "This isn't going to work," "This is a waste of time," or "I wish I could believe this but I just can't" keep you from praying and choosing the truth. Belief is a choice. If you choose to believe what you feel, then Satan, the "father of lies," will keep you in bondage. We must choose to believe what God says, regardless of what our feelings tell us. Even if it's difficult for you, pray the following prayer.

> *Dear heavenly Father, I know that You want me to face the truth and that I must be honest with You. I know that choosing to believe the truth will set me free. I have been deceived by Satan, the father of lies, and I have deceived myself as well. I thought I could hide from You, but You see everything and still love me. I pray in the name of the Lord Jesus Christ, asking You to rebuke all of Satan's demons through Him, who shed His blood and rose from the dead for me. I have trusted in Jesus alone to save me, and so I am Your child. Therefore, by the authority of the Lord Jesus Christ, I command all evil spirits to leave my pres-*

*ence. I ask the Holy Spirit to lead me into all truth. I
ask You, Father, to look deep inside me and know my
heart. Show me if there is anything in me that I am
trying to hide, because I want to be free. In Jesus'
name. Amen.*

Take some time now to let God reveal any of Satan's evil
tricks that he's used against you in your life. False teachers
and deceiving spirits can fool you, but you can also fool
yourself. Now that you are alive in Christ and forgiven, you
don't need to live a lie or defend yourself like you used to.
Christ is now your truth and defense.

Ways You Can Deceive Yourself

- *Hearing God's Word but not doing it (James 1:22;
  4:17)*
- *Saying I have no sin (1 John 1:8)*
- *Thinking I am something I'm not (Gal. 6:3)*
- *Thinking I am wise in the things of the world (1 Cor.
  3:18-19)*
- *Thinking I will not reap what I sow (Gal. 6:7)*
- *Thinking that ungodly people who live lives of sin will
  share in God's kingdom (1 Cor. 6:9)*
- *Thinking I can hang out with bad people and they
  won't have any influence on me (1 Cor. 15:33)*
- *Thinking I can be a good Christian and still hurt others
  by what I say (James 1:22)*

Use the following prayer of confession for each item
above that you have believed. Pray through each item
separately.

Lord, I confess that I have deceived myself by _____.
I thank You for Your forgiveness and commit myself to
believing Your truth.

Wrong Ways of Defending Yourself

- *Refusing to face the bad things that have happened to me (denial of reality)*
- *Escaping from the real world by daydreaming, TV, movies, computer or video games, music, etc. (fantasy)*
- *Withdrawing from people to avoid rejection (emotional isolation)*
- *Reverting (going back) to a less-threatening time of life (regression)*
- *Taking out frustrations on others (displaced anger)*
- *Blaming others for my problems (projection)*
- *Making excuses for poor behavior (rationalization)*

Use the following prayer of confession for each item above that you have participated in. Pray through each item separately.

Lord, I confess that I have defended myself wrongly by _____. I thank You for Your forgiveness and commit myself to trusting in You to defend and protect me.

Choosing the truth may be difficult if you have lived a lie and have been deceived for some time. The Christian needs only one defense, Jesus. Knowing that you are completely forgiven and accepted as God's child sets you free to face reality and declare your total dependence upon Him.

Faith is the biblical response to the truth, and believing the truth is a choice we can all make. If you say, "I want to believe God, but I just can't" you are being deceived. Of course you can believe God because what God says is always true.

Faith is something you decide to do, whether or not you feel like doing it. Believing the truth doesn't make it true, however. *It's true; therefore we believe it.*

Simply "having faith" is not the key issue here. It's what or who you believe in that makes the difference. Everybody believes in something, and everybody lives according to what he or she believes. The question is: Is the object of your faith trustworthy? If what you believe is not true, then how you live will not be right.

Read aloud the following Statement of Truth, thinking about the words as you read them. Read it every day for several weeks. This will help you renew your mind and replace any lies you have believed with the truth.

Statement of Truth

1. *I believe there is only one true and living God (Ex. 20:2-3) who is the Father, Son, and Holy Spirit. He is worthy of all honor, praise, and glory. I believe He made all things and holds all things together (Col. 1:16-17).*

2. *I recognize Jesus Christ as the Messiah, the Word who became flesh and lived with us (John 1:1, 14). I believe He came to destroy the works of the devil (1 John 3:8).*

3. *I believe that God showed His love for me by having Jesus die for me, even though I was sinful (Rom. 5:8). I believe that God rescued me from the dark power of Satan and brought me into the kingdom of His Son, who forgives my sins and sets me free (Col. 1:13-14).*

4. *I believe I am spiritually strong because Jesus is my strength. I have authority to stand against Satan because I am God's child (1 John 3:1-3). I believe I was saved by the grace of God through faith, that it was a gift and not the result of any works of mine (Eph. 2:8-9).*

5. *I choose to be strong in the Lord and in the strength of His might (Eph. 6:10). I put no confidence in the flesh (Phil. 3:3) because my weapons of spiritual bat-*

tle are not of the flesh but are powerful through God for the tearing down of Satan's strongholds (2 Cor. 10:4). I put on the whole armor of God (Eph. 6:10-20), and I resolve to stand firm in my faith and resist the evil one (1 Peter 5:8-9).

6. *I believe that apart from Christ I can do nothing (John 15:5), yet I can do all things through Him who strengthens me (Phil. 4:13). Therefore, I choose to rely totally on Christ. I choose to abide in Christ in order to bear much fruit and glorify the Lord (John 15:8). I announce to Satan that Jesus is my Lord (1 Cor. 12:3), and I reject any counterfeit gifts or works of Satan in my life.*

7. *I believe that the truth will set me free (John 8:32). I stand against Satan's lies by taking every thought captive in obedience to Christ (2 Cor. 10:5). I believe that the Bible is the only reliable guide for my life (2 Tim. 3:15-16). I choose to speak the truth in love (Eph. 4:15).*

8. *I choose to present my body as an instrument of righteousness, a living and holy sacrifice, and to renew my mind with God's Word (Rom. 6:13; 12:1-2). I put off the old self with its evil practices and put on the new self (Col. 3:9-10). I am a new creation in Christ (2 Cor. 5:17).*

9. *I ask my Heavenly Father to direct my life and to give me power to live by the Holy Spirit (Eph. 5:18), so that He can guide me into all truth (John 16:13). He will give me strength to live above sin and not carry out the desires of my flesh. I crucify the flesh, choose to be led by the Holy Spirit and to obey Him (Gal. 5:16, 24).*

10. *I renounce all selfish goals and choose the greatest goal of love (1 Tim. 1:5). I choose to obey the two greatest commandments to love the Lord my God*

with all my heart, soul, and mind, and to love my neighbor as myself (Matt. 22:37-39).

11. *I believe that Jesus has all authority in heaven and on earth (Matt. 28:18) and that He rules over everything (Col. 2:10). I believe that Satan and his demons have been defeated by Christ and are subject to me since I am a member of Christ's body (Eph. 1:19-20; 2:6). So, I obey the command to submit to God and to resist the devil (James 4:7) and I command Satan, by the authority of the Lord Jesus Christ, to leave my presence.*

Step 3: Bitterness Versus Forgiveness

When you fail to forgive those who hurt you, you become a wide-open target for Satan. God commands us to forgive others as we have been forgiven (Eph. 4:32). You need to obey this command so that Satan can't take advantage of you (2 Cor. 2:11). Christians are to forgive others and show them mercy because our Heavenly Father has shown mercy to us. Ask God to bring to your mind the names of those people you need to forgive by praying the following prayer out loud. (Remember to let this prayer come from your heart as well as your mouth!)

Dear Heavenly Father, I thank You for Your great kindness and patience which has led me to turn from my sins (Rom. 2:4). I know I have not been completely kind, patient, and loving toward those who have hurt me. I have had bad thoughts and feelings toward them. I ask You to bring to my mind all the people I need to forgive (Matt. 18:35). I ask You to bring to the surface all my painful memories so that I can choose to forgive these people from my heart. I pray this in

*the precious name of Jesus who has forgiven me and
who will heal me from my hurts. Amen.*

On a sheet of paper, make a list of the people who come
to your mind. At this point, don't question whether you
need to forgive a certain person or not. If a name comes to
your mind, write it down.

Finally, write "me" at the bottom of the list. Forgiving
yourself means accepting God's cleansing and forgiveness.
Also, write "thoughts against God." We sometimes harbor
angry thoughts toward God.

We can expect or even demand that He act in a certain
way in our lives, and when He doesn't do what we want in
the way we want, we can get angry. Those feelings can
become a wall between us and God, and even though we
don't actually need to forgive Him because He is perfect,
we do need to let the feelings go.

Before you begin working through the process of forgiving the people on your list, stop and consider what real
forgiveness is and what it is not.

Forgiveness is not forgetting. People who would like to
forget all their pain before they get around to forgiving
someone, usually find they cannot. God commands us to
forgive now. Confusion sometimes arises about this because
Scripture says that God will remember our sins no more
(Heb. 10:17). But God knows everything and can't "forget"
as if He had no memory of our sin. God promises to never
use your past against you (Ps. 103:10). And so, you may not
be able to forget your past, but you can be free from it by
forgiving others. When we bring up the past and use it
against others, we are showing that we have not yet forgiven
them (Mark 11:25).

Forgiveness is a choice, a decision of the will. Since God
requires us to forgive, it is something we can do. Forgiveness
seems hard because it pulls against our sense of what is right

and fair. We naturally want revenge for the things we have suffered. But we are told by God never to take our own revenge (Rom. 12:19).

You might be thinking, "Why should I let them off the hook?" And that is exactly the problem. As long as you do not forgive, you are still hooked to those who hurt you. You are still chained to your past. *By forgiving, you let them off your hook, but they are not off God's hook.* We must trust Him to deal with the other person justly, fairly, and mercifully, something we cannot do.

You say, "But you don't know how much this person hurt me." But until you let go of your hate and anger, they will continue to be able to hurt you. You finally stop the pain by forgiving them. You forgive for your sake, so that you can be free. *Forgiveness is mainly an issue of obedience between you and God.* God wants you to be free; this is the only way.

Forgiveness is agreeing to live with the consequences of another person's sin. Forgiveness costs you something. You choose to pay the price for the evil you forgive. But you will live with the consequences whether you want to or not. Your only choice is whether you will do so in the bondage of bitterness or in the freedom of forgiveness.

Of course, Jesus took the eternal consequences of all sin upon Himself. God "made him who had no sin to be sin for us, so that in him we might become the righteousness of God" (2 Cor. 5:21). We need, however, to accept the temporary consequences of what was done to us. But no one truly forgives without suffering the pain of another's sin. That can seem unfair and we wonder, where is the justice? It is found at the cross which makes forgiveness legally and morally right. As those who crucified Jesus mocked and jeered, Jesus prayed, "Father, forgive them for they do not know what they are doing" (Luke 23:34).

How do you forgive from your heart? You allow God to

bring to the surface the mental agony, emotional pain, and feelings of hurt toward those who hurt you. If your forgiveness doesn't reach down to the emotional core of your life, it will be incomplete. Too often we try to bury the pain inside us, making it hard to get in touch with how we really feel. Though we may not know how to or even want to bring our feelings to the surface, God does. Let God bring the pain to the surface so that He can deal with it. This is where God's gentle healing process begins.

Forgiveness is the decision not to use that offense against them. It is not unusual for us to remember a past, hurtful event and find the anger and hate we felt returning. It is tempting to bring up the issue with the one who hurt us in order to make them feel bad. But we must choose to take that thought of revenge captive to the obedience of Christ, and choose to maintain forgiveness.

This doesn't mean you must continue to put up with the future sins of others. God does not tolerate sin and neither should you. Nor should you put yourself in the position of being continually abused and hurt by the sins of others. You need to take a stand against sin while continuing to forgive those who hurt you.

Don't wait to forgive until you feel like forgiving. You will never get there. Your emotions will begin to heal, once you have obeyed God's command to forgive. Satan will have lost his power over you in that area, and God's healing touch will take over. For now, it is freedom that will be gained, not necessarily a feeling.

As you pray, God may bring to mind painful memories you had totally forgotten. Let Him do this, even if it hurts. God wants to free you; forgiving these people is the only way. Don't try to excuse the offender's behavior, even if it is someone close to you.

Remember, forgiveness is dealing with your own pain and leaving the other person to deal with God. Good feelings will follow in time. Freeing yourself from the past is the critical issue right now.

Don't say, "Lord, please help me to forgive." He is already helping you and will be with you all the way through the process. Don't say, "Lord, I want to forgive" because that bypasses the hard choice we have to make. Say, "Lord, I forgive." As you move down your list, stay with each individual until you are sure you have dealt with all the remembered pain, everything the person did that hurt you, and how it made you feel (rejected, unloved, unworthy, dirty, etc.).

It's time to begin. For each person on your list, pray aloud:

> Lord, I forgive (name the person) for (what they did to hurt you) even though it made me feel (the painful memories or feelings).

Once you have dealt with every offense that has come to your mind and you have honestly expressed how that person hurt you, then conclude by praying:

> Lord, I choose not to hold any of these things against (name) any longer. I thank You for setting me free from the bondage of my bitterness toward (name). I choose now to ask You to bless (name). In Jesus' name. Amen.

Step 4: Rebellion Versus Submission

We live in rebellious times. Often young people today don't respect people that God has placed in positions of authority over them. You may have a problem living in submission to authority. You can easily be deceived into thinking that those in authority over you are robbing you of your freedom. In reality, however, God has placed them there for your protection.

Rebelling against God and His authorities is serious business. It gives Satan an opportunity to attack you. Submission is the only solution. God requires more of you, however, than just the outward appearance of submission. He wants you to sincerely submit to your authorities, especially parents, from the heart. When you submit, your commanding general, the Lord Jesus Christ, is telling you to "Get into ranks and follow Me!" He promises that He will not lead you into temptation, but will deliver you from the evil one (Matt. 6:13).

The Bible makes it clear that we have two main responsibilities toward those in authority over us: to pray for them and submit to them. Pray the following prayer out loud from your heart.

Dear heavenly Father, You have said in the Bible that rebellion is the same thing as witchcraft, and being self-willed is like serving false gods (1 Sam. 15:23). I know that I have disobeyed and rebelled in my heart against You and those You have placed in authority over me. I thank You for Your forgiveness for my rebellion. I pray that You will show me all the ways I have been rebellious. I choose to adopt a submissive spirit and servant's heart. In Jesus' precious name I pray. Amen.

Placing ourselves under authority is an act of faith! By submitting, we are trusting God to work through His lines of authority.

At times parents, teachers, and other authority figures may abuse their authority and break the laws which are ordained by God for the protection of innocent people. In those cases, you need to seek help from a higher authority for your protection. The laws in your state may require you to report such abuse to the police or other protective agencies.

If there is continuing abuse (physical, mental, emotional, or sexual) at home, counseling may be needed to change this situation.

If authorities abuse their position by asking you to break God's law or compromise your commitment to Him, you need to obey God rather than man (Acts 4:19-20).

We are all told to submit to one another out of reverence for Christ (Eph. 5:21). In addition, however, God uses specific lines of authority to protect us and give order to our daily lives.

- Civil government (including traffic laws, drinking laws, etc.) (Rom. 13:1-7; 1 Tim. 2:1-4; 1 Peter 2:13-17)
- Parents, steparents, or legal guardians (Eph. 6:1-3)
- Teachers, coaches, and school officials (Rom. 13:1-4)
- Your boss (Rom. 13:1-4)
- Husband (Eph. 5:22-24)
- Church leaders (pastor, youth pastor, Sunday school teacher) (Heb. 13:17)
- God Himself (Daniel 9:5, 9)

Examine each of the seven areas of authority listed above and ask the Lord to forgive you for those times you have not respected these positions or submitted to them, by praying:

Lord, I agree with You that I have been rebellious toward _____. Please forgive me for this rebellion. I choose to be submissive and obedient to Your Word. In Jesus' name. Amen.

Step 5: Pride Versus Humility _____

Pride is a killer. Pride says, "I can do it! I can get myself out of this mess without God or anyone else's help." Oh no, we can't! We absolutely need God, and we desperately need each other. Paul wrote, "We . . . worship by the Spirit of God . . . glory in Christ Jesus, and . . . put no confidence in the flesh" (Phil. 3:3).

Humility is confidence properly placed in God. We are to be "strong in the Lord, and in the strength of His might" (Eph. 6:10 NASB). James 4:6-10 and 1 Peter 5:1-10 tell us that spiritual problems will follow when we are proud. Use the following prayer to express your commitment to live humbly before God.

Dear heavenly Father, You have said that pride goes before destruction and a haughty spirit before a fall (Prov. 16:18). I confess that I have been thinking mainly of myself and not of others. I have not denied myself, picked up my cross daily, and followed You (Matt. 16:24), and as a result, I have given ground to the enemy in my life. I have believed that I could be successful by living according to my own power and resources. I now confess that I have sinned against You by placing my will before Yours and by centering my life around myself instead of You. I renounce my pride and my selfishness and close any doors I've opened in my life or my physical body to the enemies of the Lord Jesus Christ. I choose to rely on the Holy Spirit's power and guidance so that I can do Your will. I give my heart to You and stand against all of Satan's attacks. I ask You to show me how to live for others. I now choose to make others more important than myself and to make You the most important of all in my life (Rom. 12:10; Matt. 6:33). Please show

me specifically now the ways in which I have lived
pridefully. I ask this in the name of my Lord Jesus
Christ. Amen.

Having made that commitment in prayer, now allow God to show you any specific areas of your life where you have been prideful, such as:

- I have a stronger desire to do my will than to do God's will.
- I rely on my own strengths and abilities rather than on God's.
- I too often think my ideas are better than other people's ideas.
- I want to control how others act rather than develop self-control.
- I sometimes consider myself more important than others.
- I have a tendency to think I don't need other people.
- I find it difficult to admit when I am wrong.
- I am more likely to be a people-pleaser than a God-pleaser.
- I am overly concerned about getting credit for doing good things.
- I often think I am more humble than others.
- I often think I am smarter than my parents.
- I often feel my needs are more important than others' needs.
- I consider myself better than others because of my academic, artistic, or athletic abilities and accomplishments.

For each of the above areas that have been true in your life, pray out loud:

Lord, I agree I have been prideful in the area of _____.
Thank You for forgiving me for this pridefulness. I
choose to humble myself and place all my confidence in
You. Amen.

Step 6: Bondage Versus Freedom _____

The next step to freedom deals with the sins that have
become habits in your life. If you have been caught in the
vicious cycle of "sin-confess-sin-confess," realize that the
road to victory is "sin-confess-*resist*" (James 4:7). Habitual
sin often requires help from a trusted brother or sister in
Christ. James 5:16 says, "Confess your sins to each other
and pray for each other so that you may be healed. The
effective prayer of a righteous man is powerful and effective." Seek out a stronger Christian who will lift you up in
prayer and hold you accountable in your areas of weakness.

Sometimes the assurance of 1 John 1:9 is sufficient: "If
we confess our sins, he is faithful and just and will forgive
us our sins and purify us from all unrighteousness."

Remember, confession is not saying, "I'm sorry"; it's
openly admitting, "I did it." Whether you need the help of
others or just the accountability of God, pray the following
prayer out loud:

Dear heavenly Father, You have told us to put on the
Lord Jesus Christ and make no provision for the flesh
in regard to its lust (Rom. 13:14 NASB). I agree that I
have given in to sinful desires which wage war
against my soul (1 Peter 2:11). I thank You that in
Christ my sins are forgiven, but I have broken Your
holy law and given the devil an opportunity to wage
war in my body (Rom. 6:12-13; James 4:1; 1 Peter
5:8). I come before Your presence now to admit these
sins and to seek Your cleansing (1 John 1:9) that I

may be freed from the bondage of sin. I now ask You to reveal to my mind the ways that I have broken Your moral law and grieved the Holy Spirit. In Jesus' precious name I pray. Amen.

There are many habitual sins that can control us. The following list contains some of the more common sins of the flesh. Look through the list and ask the Holy Spirit to reveal to your mind which ones you need to confess. He may bring to mind others that are not here. For each one God reveals, pray the following prayer of confession from your heart.

- stealing
- lying
- fighting
- hatred
- jealousy and envy
- anger
- complaining and criticism
- impure thoughts
- eagerness for lustful pleasure
- perfectionism
- cheating
- gossiping
- procrastination (putting things off)
- swearing
- greed and materialism
- apathy and laziness
- other

Lord, I admit that I have committed the sin of _____. I thank You for Your forgiveness and cleansing. I turn away from this sin and turn to You, Lord. Strengthen me by Your Holy Spirit to obey You. In Jesus' name. Amen.

It is our responsibility to take control over sin in our bodies. We must not use our bodies or someone else's as an instrument of unrighteousness (Rom. 6:12-13). If you are struggling with sexual sins you can't stop (such as pornography, masturbation, heavy petting, heavy kissing, oral sex, or sexual intercourse) pray as follows:

Lord, I ask You to reveal to my mind every sexual use of my body as an instrument of unrighteousness. In Jesus' precious name I pray. Amen.

As the Lord brings to your mind every sexual use of your body, whether it was done to you (i.e., rape, incest, or any sexual molestation) or willingly by you, renounce every occasion:

Lord, I renounce (name the specific use of your body) with (name the person involved) and I ask You to break that sinful bond with (name).

After you have completed this exercise, commit your body to the Lord by praying out loud from your heart:

Lord, I renounce all these uses of my body as an instrument of unrighteousness, and I admit my willful participation. Lord, I choose to present my eyes, my mouth, my mind, my hands and feet, my whole body to You as instruments of righteousness. I now present my body to You as a living sacrifice, holy and acceptable unto You, and I choose to reserve the sexual use of my body (my sexual organs) for marriage only (Heb. 13:4).
I reject the lie of Satan that my body is not clean or that it is dirty or in any way unacceptable to You as a result of my past sexual experiences. Lord, I thank You that You have totally cleansed and forgiven me, and that You love me just as I am. Therefore, I can accept myself and my body as cleansed in Your eyes. In Jesus' name. Amen.

Special Prayers for Specific Needs
Homosexual
Lord, I renounce the lie that You have created me or

anyone else to be homosexual, and I agree that You clearly forbid homosexual behavior. I accept myself as a child of God and declare that You created me a man (or a woman). I renounce all homosexual thoughts, urges, or drives, as well as any bondage of Satan, that have perverted my relationships with others. I announce that I am free to relate to the opposite sex and my own sex in the way that You intended. In Jesus' name. Amen.

Abortion

Lord, I confess that I was not a proper guardian and keeper of the life You entrusted to me, and I ask Your forgiveness. I choose to accept Your forgiveness by forgiving myself, and I now commit that child to You for Your care for all eternity. In Jesus' name. Amen.

Suicidal Tendencies

I renounce suicidal thoughts and any attempts I may have made to take my own life or in any way injure myself. I renounce the lie that life is hopeless and that I can find peace and freedom by taking my own life. Satan is a thief, and he comes to steal, kill, and destroy. I choose life in Christ who said He came to give me life and give it to the full. I choose to accept Your forgiveness by forgiving myself, and I choose to believe that there is always hope in Christ. In Jesus' name. Amen.

Eating Disorders or Cutting on Yourself

I renounce the lie that my value as a person is dependent upon my physical beauty, my weight or size. I renounce cutting myself, vomiting, using laxatives, or starving myself as a means of cleansing myself of evil or altering my appearance. I announce that only the blood of the Lord Jesus Christ cleanses me from sin. I accept the reality that there may be sin present in me due to the lies I have believed and the wrongful use of my body. But I renounce the lie that I am evil or that any part of my body is evil. My body is the temple of the Holy Spirit and I belong to God. I am totally accepted by God in Christ, just as I am. In Jesus' name. Amen.

Substance Abuse

Lord, I confess that I have misused substances (alcohol, tobacco, food, prescription or street drugs) for the purpose of pleasure, to escape reality, or to cope with difficult problems. I confess that I have abused my body and programmed my mind in a harmful way. I have not allowed Your Holy Spirit to guide me. I ask Your forgiveness, and I reject any satanic connection or influence in my life because of my misuse of drugs or food. I cast my cares onto Christ who loves me, and I commit myself to no longer give in to substance abuse, but instead allow the Holy Spirit to lead and empower me. In Jesus' name. Amen.

After you have confessed all known sin, pray:

I now confess these sins to You and claim, through the blood of the Lord Jesus Christ, my forgiveness and cleansing. I cancel all ground that evil spirits have gained through my willful involvement in sin. I ask this in the wonderful name of my Lord and Savior Jesus Christ. Amen.

Step 7: Curses Versus Blessings _____

The last step to freedom is to renounce the sins of your ancestors and any curses which may have been placed on you. In giving the Ten Commandments, God said, "You shall not make for yourself an idol, in the form of anything in heaven above or on the earth beneath or in the waters below. You shall not bow down to them or worship them; for I, the Lord your God, am a jealous God, punishing the children for the sin of the fathers to the third and fourth generation of those who hate me" (Ex. 20:4-5).

Demonic or familiar spirits can be passed on from one generation to the next, if you don't renounce the sins of your ancestors and claim your new spiritual heritage in Christ. *You are not guilty for the sin of your ancestors,* but because of their sin, Satan has gained access to your family.

In addition, deceived and evil people may try to curse you, or satanic groups may try to target you. You have all the authority and protection you need in Christ to stand against such curses. In order to walk free from the sins of your ancestors and any demonic influences, read the following declaration and pray the following prayer out loud. Let the words come from your heart as you remember the authority you have in Christ Jesus.

Declaration

I here and now reject and disown all the sins of my ancestors. As one delivered from the domain of darkness into the kingdom of God's Son, I cancel out all demonic working that was passed down to me from my family. As one who is crucified and raised with Jesus Christ and who sits with Him in heavenly places, I renounce all satanic assignments that are directed toward me. I cancel out every curse that Satan and his workers have put on me. I announce to Satan and all his forces that Christ became a curse for me (Gal. 3:13) when He died for my sins on the cross. I reject any and every way in which Satan may claim ownership of me. I belong to the Lord Jesus Christ who purchased me with His own blood. I reject all the blood sacrifices whereby Satan may claim ownership of me. I declare myself to be eternally and completely signed over and committed to the Lord Jesus Christ. By the authority that I have in Jesus Christ, I now command every familiar spirit and every enemy of the Lord Jesus Christ that is influencing me to leave my presence. I commit myself to my Heavenly Father, to do His will from this day forward.

Prayer

Dear heavenly Father, I come to You as Your child, purchased by the blood of the Lord Jesus Christ. You are the Lord of the universe and the Lord of my life. I submit my body to You as an instrument of righteousness, a living sacrifice, that I may glorify You in my body. I now ask Your Holy Spirit to lead and empower me to know and do Your will. I commit myself to the renewing of my mind in order to prove that Your will is good, perfect, and acceptable for me. All this I do in the name and authority of the Lord Jesus Christ. Amen.

Purity Pointers

Read: Galatians 5:1

Reflect:

1. Which of the Steps to Freedom seemed to help you most? Is there anything you still need to deal with?
2. Why is it the person of Christ who brings freedom and not these steps?
3. If you find yourself in bondage again can these truths help you?
4. In what way could you share this message of hope and freedom with other teens? Do you think they would listen?

Respond:

Dear heavenly Father, You said that the truth would set me free and You were right. Thank You for showing me the road to freedom in Christ. I ask You now to help me grow, as I choose to maintain my freedom. Jesus, You are the Bondage Breaker. Thank You for never giving up on me and always loving me. In Jesus' name I pray. Amen.

~~~~ Notes

Chapter Two
1. Anderson, Neil, *Walking in the Light* (Nashville, TN: Thomas Nelson, 1992), 21.

Chapter Three
1. Knapp, Martin Wells, *Impressions* (Weaton, IL: Tyndale House, 1984), 32.
2. Anderson, Neil T. and Steve Russo, *The Seduction of Our Children* (Eugene, OR: Harvest House, 1991), 34-35.

Chapter Six
1. Blackaby, Henry and Claude King, *Experiencing God* (Nashville, TN: Lifeway Press, 1990), 24-25.
2. Anderson, Neil, *Walking in the Light*, 81.

Chapter Seven
1. Anderson, Neil, *Living Free in Christ* (Ventura, CA: Regal Books, 1993).

Chapter Ten
1. Anderson, Neil, *Walking in the Light*, 138-139.

ᔰ About the Authors

Neil Anderson worked for four years as an aerospace engineer before entering the ministry. He has been a youth pastor, associate pastor, and a senior pastor. He taught at the Talbot School of Theology for ten years before founding Freedom in Christ Ministries. His ministry is known throughout the world.

Rich Miller served with Student Venture (a high school ministry of Campus Crusade for Christ) for seventeen years in the United States and the Phillipines. He also traveled with Josh McDowell for a year. He now serves as a speaker and author for Freedom in Christ Youth and Young Adult Ministries.

Freedom in Christ Conducts Conferences!

Freedom in Christ Ministries is an inter-denominational, international, Bible-teaching church ministry which exists to glorify God by equipping churches and mission groups, enabling them to fulfill their mission of establishing people free in Christ. Thousands have found their freedom in Christ; your group can too! Here are some conferences your community can host which would be led by Freedom in Christ staff:

Freedom for Leaders (a two-day conference of renewal and freedom for leaders).

Living Free in Christ (a seven-day Bible conference on resolving personal and spiritual conflicts).

Spiritual Conflicts and Counseling (a two-day advanced seminar on helping others find freedom in Christ).

Setting Your Church Free (a leadership conference on corporate freedom for churches, ministries, and mission groups).

Breaking the Chains (a young adult conference for college age, singles, and young marrieds).

Stomping Out the Darkness (a youth conference for parents, youth workers, and young people).

Setting Your Youth Free (an advanced seminar for youth pastors, youth workers, and parents).

Purity Under Pressure (a conference for teens on living a life of sexual purity).

The Seduction of Our Children (a seminar for parents and children's workers wanting to lead children to freedom in Christ).

Resolving Spiritual Conflicts and Cross-Cultural Ministry (a conference for leaders, missionaries, and all believers desiring to see the Great Commission fulfilled).

The above conferences are also available on video and audio cassettes. To order these and other resources, write or call us.

To host a conference, write us at:

Freedom in Christ
491 East Lambert Road
La Habra, CA 90631
Phone: 310-691-9128 Fax: 310-691-4035

More Resources from Neil Anderson and Freedom in Christ to help you and those you love find freedom in Christ.

Books

Victory Over the Darkness
The Bondage Breaker
Helping Others Find Freedom in Christ
Released from Bondage
Walking in the Light
A Way of Escape
Purity Under Pressure (Youth)
Setting Your Church Free
Living Free in Christ
Daily in Christ
The Seduction of Our Children
Spiritual Warfare
Stomping Out the Darkness (Youth)
The Bondage Breaker Youth Edition
To My Dear Slimeball
Know Light No Fear

Personal Study Guides

Victory Over the Darkness
    Study Guide
The Bondage Breaker
    Study Guide
Stomping Out theDarkness
    Study Guide
The Bondage Breaker Youth Edition
    Study Guide
Extreme Faith
    Youth Devotional

Teaching Study Guides

Breaking Through to Spiritual Maturity
    (Group Study)
Helping Others Find Freedom in Christ
    (Study Guide)
Busting Free
    (Youth Group Study)